M000307810

WALKING WITH ANGELS

A STORY OF DIVINE INTERVENTION AND THE MEMOIRS OF RAYMOND C. SIMON, CRIMINOLOGIST

RAYMOND C. SIMON

with

KIMBERLY GERBER SPINA

R&J Books

Cover Design: Al Mahmud Didar
mahmuddidar21@gmail.com

Cover Photograph: Marian Miller/Hudson Photography
http://www.nhudsonphoto.com

Coauthor Photograph: Al Spina
https://www.PointClickPost.com

Digital Formatting: Austin Brown
austinjackbrown@gmail.com

ISBN (Hardcover Version): 978-0-578-29863-4
ISBN (Digital Version): 978-0-578-29862-7

v.090622

CONTENTS

DEDICATION

*"The greatest legacy one can pass on to one's
children and grandchildren
is not money, but rather
a legacy of character and faith."*
Billy Graham

Rather than leave this earth without my family
and loved ones having knowledge of my life,
I resolved to write my memoirs
which I dedicate to my wife Joan,
son Jeff Simon & his wife Tuesday Van Dyke Simon,
daughter Julie Simon Avery & her husband Greg Avery;
grandchildren Matthew, Cameron, and
Courtney Avery Piearcy newly married to John Piearcy;
Jessica Simon Vella & her husband Dan Vella,
Christian Simon and Corbin Simon,
great-grandchildren Harper Rae and Walker Hunter Vella,
ad infinitum for the history of the Simon Family.

Lovingly composed,
Raymond C. Simon

INTRODUCTION

Divine Beings walk among us, and we aren't always aware of their presence until (and often even after) their intervention rescues us from impending disaster. Being saved by a stranger from almost drowning in a lake during a fierce and sudden storm, surviving a near-catastrophic fire inflight aboard a military aircraft during the Korean war, and an unexpected delay that prevented me from boarding a helicopter that crashed, killing everyone aboard moments after takeoff are only a few examples of what can only be described as divine interventions from the angels who constantly guide and protect us.

This is a story about a boy from Conrad, Montana who has experienced many fantastic adventures and a good number of providential events throughout his life. I believe this story will provide some entertainment for my grand-children, children, and friends, and may be very helpful to others — especially the fact that many of the interventions that came my way allowed me to live to this ripe old age. Oh yes, that young boy is still alive, and this is what has allowed him to write this story.

What is divine intervention? Frankly, I'm not certain, but I do have several thoughts on the subject. What we do know about it is that it comes from God and, in turn, Jesus Christ.

To me, it seems impractical to believe that with billions of people on earth, God is able to answer every prayer himself, which explains why there are angels and archangels. Without a doubt, innumerable divine beings receive our prayers.

Just how do they intervene? I believe it's possible they intercede in an infinite number of ways. For instance, I don't believe that if you are ill, an archangel comes down and touches you and instantly cures you. However, you can have thoughts dropped into your mind or in some other person's mind regarding your needs at a critical time. Those thoughts can then translate into actions by others, unknown even to themselves, that would lead to help for you in some way, either physical or mental. There is power in prayer, and untold numbers of people have witnessed this in their own experiences.

I believe that circumstances happen in strange ways through angels that can cause a situation to change, and that every angel operates in harmony with God, and in our heart, mind, body and soul. The purpose of this story is simply to share with you the number of times in my life

I've had angels intervene. They have allowed me to go on living out of harm's way, and in a blessed life I could never have imagined.

—Raymond C. Simon

PREFACE

This is the exciting and inspiring true story of many divine interventions; a journey of walking the path of life with angels.

At the wonderful age of 90 I had been asked to write my memoirs, and so I weave into this story my good fortune of the people I have met and experiences that changed my life, and the five times I nearly lost my life but was saved by divine intervention; evidence that I have my whole life walked with God's angels.

Born to parents who weathered World War I and The Great Depression, I was fortunate to grow up in a family full of love and support. I was blessed with a beautiful singing voice and won my first singing contest at the age of five. At the age of seven I was singing in bars thanks to the instigation of older siblings, and when I was 12 years old I had the good luck of being able to perform with the famous movie star Ethel Barrymore, traveling to military bases on the West Coast. These are memories I will always treasure.

Military experience taught me to appreciate the unforeseen gifts one can stumble onto in the midst of a war, along with unavoidable horrors and the unexpected chance for survival.

While working as a graduate criminologist I witnessed the darkest side of humanity, and was rescued by unseen forces when I came face to face with imminent death. Self-preservation influenced me to change my vocation.

Moving back to Modesto presented me with a fantastic job opportunity to work as an investigator for Freese & Gianelli, a local insurance adjusting firm. Bud Gianelli and I hit it off and again to my great fortune I was in the right place at the right time, and this career lasted over 50 years.

Once we were settled in our community I was invited into local politics and again was blessed with many experiences that, when I look back on my life, I can hardly believe really happened. Traveling the globe, dining in world renowned restaurants, befriended by a Michelin Star French Chef in Florence, Italy, and being a guest at the Emperor Maximilian and Empress Carlota's castle are just a few extraordinary life experiences put in my path.

There are two specific transcendent encounters in my life which I found unexplainable. One of them involved my sister Jeanne.

When my mother passed away it was my responsibility to notify all of my brothers and sisters of her passing. I was somewhat worried about talking to my sister Jeanne because during my life when we were both living at home, she argued almost incessantly with our mother, Etta. They were always butting heads and as a child it was quite frightening for me.

When I called and told Jeanne the terrible news, she started sobbing. She was inconsolable and it went on for quite some time. I finally interrupted her and explained about Mother's death and could she come to the funeral.

She answered, "Yes, Ray. I'm just on my knees praying that God will take care of my mother."

Jeanne did come for the funeral, and once all of my brothers and sisters had arrived in Modesto I planned a pre-funeral get together at my house. We made arrangements the next day to go to the funeral home together and I dreaded that because I didn't know how everyone would react, especially Jeanne.

When we got there, Jeanne was first in line to view our mother, and she had the most placid, pleasant smile on her face; she looked quite peaceful about the whole thing, not at all like I had imagined. On the contrary, my other sister Mary was almost out of control sobbing and was difficult to console.

After the funeral the next day Joan and I hosted a reception in our home which everyone attended. I said to Jeanne, "I am pleased and surprised that you seemed so peaceful during the viewing and funeral. What happened?"

She told me, "Ray, when I heard the news that Mother had passed, I couldn't stop sobbing. I fell to my knees at my bedside and cried and cried. At some point I felt something wash over me, a calm that just made me feel suddenly at peace. I looked up to the corner of my room and there was a beautiful outline of my mother; she looked to be in her 20s. It was a little fuzzy, but I could tell it was her.

"I heard Mother's voice then. She said to me, 'Jeanne, do not worry. Everything is forgiven and I'm so happy, so very happy.' There was a figure standing beside her, a tall man, and he said, 'Come on Etta, it's time to go.'"

Well, I would never have thought that my first affirmation regarding angels would come from such an unlikely source, especially considering the volatile relationship I had witnessed between Jeanne and our mother all those years growing up in the same house. It really was a beautiful gift that my mother gave my sister, and that my sister in the telling of her experience gave to me.

The next occurrence was after my second hospitalization. Having been moved to a rehabilitation hospital, I became seriously ill and was fading fast. The doctor basically dismissed my symptoms as the flu. Fortunately my son Jeff intervened and insisted they transfer me immediately by ambulance back to the hospital. He then called my doctor to meet us at Memorial.

After a brief conversation with Dr. Forester, he instantly diagnosed me — he told Jeff I had developed giant cell temporal arteritis. The very same thing had happened to his father twenty years earlier.

Oblivious of all that had transpired during this period, I eventually woke up, alone in my hospital bed at Memorial Hospital. Not having any idea where I was, as I looked around the room I was absolutely certain that I had been transferred to the Carmelite Monastery hospital in Carmel.

There was an open door from my room to another where two ladies sat at a small table dressed like the Carmelite nuns in their formal brown dress and habits.

I saw that they were eating breakfast and thought to myself *'I'm so hungry, I wonder if I could come in and eat?'* and as though they heard me, they waved me in. I said to them, "I can't. I can't walk," and I really couldn't.

I looked around my room and saw a very large iron Gothic cross and said to myself, *'Now there is no doubt; I've been transferred to a monastery.'* Also there were numerous plaques on every wall with Latin written on them.

The door opened up and in came my nurse, who indicated his name was Paul. I asked him, "Paul, where have you been?" He told me he'd been on vacation and had just returned. I said, "I want to ask you a question.

"Over the door do you see a Gothic cross, and the two ladies in the room there – well, they're gone now..."

Paul simply answered me, "No."

Needless to say, I was stunned because I had definitely seen everything very clearly.

This vision reinforced everything I believed. Soon after, I fell into a deep and relaxed sleep.

Whether it was the Carmelite nuns, my guiding angel, or the doctor's infusion, that was the end of my illness.

To my great fortune, my team of angels has continued to guide and protect me to this remarkable age. And so it is with immense delight that I share with family, friends, and those I do not yet know, my life story with emphasis on my absolute understanding that for some reason God's light has shined upon me and given me so much to be grateful for, including the writing of this book in which I have reached out and touched the purpose of my life!

—Raymond C. Simon

FOREWORD

Angels, the great archangels, spirit guides, saints, and beings of light that know and love us are all around us. Sometimes we call to them in a moment of despair, other times we find ourselves inexplicably saved from impending disaster, and still there might be other occasions where we are led to grand experiences that must have been orchestrated from a higher power. Whether we are gifted with the ability to see, hear, or feel their presence, we all know someone who's been blessed with these ethereal encounters.

As a longtime friend of Ray's, I've been enthralled with his exciting career history, political prowess, exceptional good fortune, and especially his seemingly inexplicable narrow escapes from catastrophe.

His fascinating experiences, which include sharing lunch – albeit unknowingly at the time – with the notorious American bank robber Pretty Boy Floyd; being educated by some of the most interesting and famous instructors in the world, including the chief psychiatrist at the Nuremberg Trials; narrowly escaping death more than once; and an occurrence in which he felt God's presence and could see and communicate with what must have been angels or his spirit guides, letting Ray know they were there to comfort him, and the message was *You will be alright*.

As you read Ray's narrative you will see that he has been surrounded by angels and beings of light from a very young age and continues to be visited and protected by these guardian angels, even today still adding to his story.

—Kimberly Gerber Spina

1

FAMILY

My father, Dave Simon, was born in Jamaica, Iowa, and lived to the ripe old age of ninety-nine. My mother, Henrietta (née Bruce) Simon, was born in Sheridan, Wyoming in 1899, and lived to the age of seventy-six.

One year Joan and I were on a Rhine River cruise and the cruise director told me that in England my last name Simon was hyphenated, that it would have been Simon-Davies. My mother told me that my father's family dropped "Davies" when they came to America, so I suppose it could be true.

I grew up in a family of eight: four boys, two girls, plus our mother and father. Conrad, Montana is a small town about ninety miles from Great Falls and not too far from Glacier National Park. The town had probably no more than ten thousand people, but we enjoyed every convenience, public and private, of that time for a city that size.

My paternal grandparents were George and Mary (née

Erickson) Simon. Grandma Mary's father, Toleff Erickson, and Grandpa George came from Wales; his family wanted to start a brick factory in Iowa. My dad said that they lived in a grass covered shack while the factory was being built.

He told me a story once about a mountain lion that tried to scratch his way through the sod roof, terrifying everyone within. Thank goodness it never got in! He also said at one point in his young life he got sick with something and was in bed for a year, with only his mother treating him.

They seemed to be doing well for a while. However, the factory burned down after a couple of years and my grandparents decided to move to Montana and finally settled in Bridger, where my grandfather went to work in the coal mines. There were six children in his family, and my dad and his brothers also worked in the coal mines. My grandfather told him one day, "Dave, you'd better find work elsewhere, or you will die in the mine."

My father went to school up until the eighth grade. At this time in America families relied on their children to help with the family farm, work in the mines, or whatever was necessary to survive. For this reason, many children did not have the opportunity to continue their education at a high- or normal-school.

Dad was good at mathematics and often helped the teacher coach the other children in school. I've always wondered what more Dad could have achieved had he been able to continue his education, but it turns out the eighth grade was quite an accomplishment at that time. In 1895 the eighth grade final exam had to be completed in five hours as is shown in the original, now well-known document which has been shared by the Smoky Valley Genealogical Society and Library in Salina, Kansas, then reprinted by the Salina Journal Newspaper. I thank Melanie Allewelt Hoff -- the daughter of my friend Bill Allewelt -- for revealing this illuminating information with me, albeit circuitously.

I've included it in the back of this chapter.

I believe the year was about 1916 or 1917 -- World War I was coming about and my father decided he wanted to join the Army, specifically the cavalry, and he started out as a private first class. After a year or so he had been promoted to sergeant major, the highest noncom (noncommissioned officer) you could be. He was then appointed lieutenant by General Pershing and joined the Black Horse Brigade: the 11th Armored Cavalry Regiment – a regiment of horses and men. I remember him telling me, "We chased Pancho Villa all over Arizona and New Mexico and down to the Mexican border." When he was transferred to his army station in Seattle, Washington for discharge, he met my mother, Henrietta Bruce. After courting for a while, they married.

My father and mother then moved to Oil Mont, Montana, where my father's brother Bill talked him into purchasing a trench digger and going to work in Cut Bank digging trenches that extended from the oil platforms to the oil terminals. They both made a fortune. It was not until 1929, the year of the Great Depression, that they lost money and had to look for other work. I know they were considered wealthy at the time because my father had bought my mother a Stutz Bearcat convertible, which back then cost $15,000. That would be equivalent to about $247,000 today.

———

My maternal great-grandparents were Charles E.B. and Mary Almira (née George) Wheeler, and my maternal grandparents were Jim and Myrtle Violetta (née Wheeler) Bruce. Grandmother Myrtle married my grandfather Jim Bruce when she was still quite young and had my mother, Etta, at the age of 16.

My mother's background was somewhat traumatic; she had a rather rough time as a child having suffered a devastating event at a very early age. As the story goes, my grandfather Jim was a railroad engineer with the Yellowstone Valley Railroad Company, a shortline railroad in northeastern Montana which ran for just 171 miles. He was gone a lot, and my grandmother, Myrtle, was left home alone quite often raising their two children — my mom Henrietta and her younger brother Robert. My grandmother would have been about 21 at this time.

Apparently, Grandpa Jim had left a pistol with Grandma Myrtle so she could protect herself since, because of his work, he was often gone for long periods of time. One day Grandma Myrtle was startled by what she thought was someone coming in through the door downstairs. She took the pistol and walked to the head of the stairwell. My mother, Henrietta, was five years old and standing with her. It's hard to know exactly what took place next.

It is believed that in her confusion and fright, my Grandmother Myrtle fell on the staircase and the gun went off. However it happened, she died from this catastrophic incident. My mother, at that young age, was a witness to all of this and was made to go to court and describe in as much detail as she could what she had seen.

The trauma my mother must have suffered from this experience definitely scarred her, and she never did talk about it in our family. My uncle was too young to remember anything about it at all.

Grandpa Jim was so distraught by this horrific event, my Grandma Myrtle's death, that he left for Seattle, Washington, leaving my mother and her little brother behind. The children were removed from the home and placed with a temporary guardian, to be taken care of until a relative could be summoned.

In his despair my grandfather began drinking heavily, and at some point, while still in Seattle he was hit by a trolley car and killed. Later in life, at my first job after college I had access to the city's archives and I searched for that story. I did find it, and sure enough, that is exactly how my grandfather James Bruce met his demise.

My maternal great-grandmother Mary Wheeler, my grandmother Myrtle Bruce's mother, lived in Vermont on a rather large and successful maple-syrup tree farm that she and my great-grandfather Charles Wheeler owned. They also owned a farming enterprise on the Isle of Lamont near Canada.

My great-grandfather had passed away at a fairly young age, and my great-grandmother Mary was left to operate the farm. When she learned of her daughter's death and the court's custody order she arrived rather quickly. She knew she had to sell the Vermont ranch and move to Montana, to rescue her grandchildren who were now orphaned. In fact, her properties were still being sold when she picked the children up in Billings, Montana. Why she decided to move to Montana instead of bringing them back to Vermont to live in her home there, we may never know.

My great-grandmother Mary was a very interesting and accomplished woman. When she made that move to Montana in the mid 1880s she bought a rather large home not too far from the Crow reservation. At this time the Crow tribe's main food sources, especially bison, were almost extinct and the Crow found that they depended more and more on Government provisions.

With her household staff, my great-grandmother took it upon herself to cook for the Crow tribe because she could see they were nearly starving to death. Every day, she would get into a wagon with her crew and the food they had prepared, and travel to the reservation to feed the Crow people.

In the process, she became good friends with the leader of the Mountain Crows of the Crow Nation: Chief Plenty Coups. I was told that he was especially fond of my mother, Etta, who would have been quite young still, maybe nine or 10 years old at that time, and at some point (as the story was passed down to us) he performed the traditional cutting of wrists with her: he cut his wrist and my mother's, and pressed their wrists together to make her an honorary Crow. It was a mysterious and profound ritual that meant a lot to my mother and her grandmother.

Chief Plenty Coups, whose name we were always told meant Many Wars or Many Achievements, was a well-known and admired man. He is recognized as one of the last great American Indian chiefs, and on March 3, 1932 his death pronounced the end of a remarkable era. He was among the last of the Indigenous American chiefs who was elected by other chiefs, and was considered a visionary. As a Crow warrior he fought against the Sioux and Cheyenne. Overall, his astonishing life and great wisdom were revered equally in war and peace.

Chief Plenty Coups was awarded a spectacular honor recognizing lives lost in WWI. According to the United States Army Arlington National Cemetery website, "Because of his high standing as a leader and diplomat, the Army invited Plenty Coups to attend the funeral of the Unknown Soldier on November 11, 1921."

"Plenty Coups' presence at the Unknown Soldier's burial was especially meaningful in light of American Indians' military service during World War I. Between 8,000 and 15,000 American Indians served during the war, even though many (one historian estimates more than a third) did not have U.S. citizenship rights at the time. Moreover, American Indian service members died at comparatively high rates during the war, because so many served in the infantry. It is possible, then, that the Unknown shared Plenty Coups' ancestry or that of another tribe. Indeed, Joseph K. Dixon stated this explicitly in his October 1921 letter to Secretary of War Joseph W. Weeks, in which he proposed that an American Indian chief participate in the Unknown's funeral ceremony. 'What more fitting than that this race of people ... should have a place in the ceremony, for doubtless hundreds of unknown Indian graves are scattered from the sea to the Alps?' Dixon wrote. 'It will give added distinction to the ceremony—the fact that the First American Warrior should lay his tribute on the grave of the Latest Hero of War—an Unknown American Soldier.'"

To pay distinct tribute to the Unknown Soldier's service and sacrifice, Chief Plenty Coups bequeathed his coup stick which held great significance to the Great Plains tribes and was exceedingly revered, as well as his feathered headdress (war bonnet) and lance. This generous and selfless act is a perpetual and poignant reminder of the many Indigenous Americans who served and sacrificed alongside the United States Military troops in World War I.

The Chief was so grateful to my great-grandmother Mary and my mother for helping his tribe, that in 1912 he presented my great-grandmother with a pair of Crow tribal war dance moccasin covers for my mother Etta. My sister Mary, who is still alive at 101, and I each still have one mate of the pair.

The moccasin covers are made of deer hide and are intricately decorated with beautiful colored beads. These were tied over their regular moccasins whenever the Crows held a war dance. I was always enthralled with this story, and still have the moccasin covers in a place of honor in my home, framed for historical preservation; one for my sister Mary and one for myself, both with a plate inscribed:

MOCCASIN COVER
CHIEF PLENTY COUPS
CROW INDIANS
Given to
Etta Bruce Simon
1912
Sheridan Wyoming

My mother would have been about 13 years old at the time she was given this great gift. This bit of Simon family history so fascinated me that I continued to collect many Indigenous American items, including an oil painting by Gene Speck titled Crow Camp, of a Crow woman and her husband. In it they are standing in front of a teepee cooking over a fire in an open field. I was in Coeur d'Alene, Idaho, at a convention when the shop containing a number of oil paintings was closing, and I asked the owner how much the painting would cost me.

He said, "I will sell it to you for $1,200. It's worth $2,000."

Being nearly twenty-five years ago, I had to say, "I'm not sure I can afford that."

He said, "You don't have to worry. I will let you pay it off to me directly by the month. I'll give you my address."

Subsequently, about four years ago, I was walking down a street in San Francisco and passed a shop that had the identical painting, only in a smaller size. I went into the shop and asked the lady how much my painting would be worth, and she told me to mail her a copy of the picture. I did and received in return a letter that if she held the painting in her shop at this time, it would be worth approximately $25,000. That was the best purchase I ever made in my life.

Later, I bought two smaller paintings by the same artist, Gene Speck, from the same lady, which are both of cowboys from that same time period. Speck is considered one of the greatest Western artists in the world. He is one of a number of famous artists who captured Indigenous Americans' encampments of the 1800s in his nostalgic paintings.

Ray's mother, Etta May Bruce (1914)

Ray's father, David Lawrence Simon (1914)

Ray's mother, Etta May Bruce Simon (1963)

Ray's father, David Lawrence Simon (1963)

EXAMINATION GRADUATION
QUESTIONS
Of SALINE COUNTY, KANSAS
April 13, 1895
J.W. ARMSTRONG, County Superintendent

Examinations at Salina, Cambria, Gypsum City, Assaria, Falun, Bavaria, and District No. 74 (in Glendale Twp.)

READING AND PENMANSHIP — The Examination will be oral, and the Penmanship of Applicants will be graded from the manuscripts.

GRAMMAR
(Time, one hour)

1. Give nine rules for the use of Capital Letters.
2. Name the Parts of Speech and define those that have no modifications.
3. Define, Verse, Stanza and Paragraph.
4. What are the Principal Parts of a verb? Give Principal Parts of do, lie, lay and run.
5. Define Case. Illustrate each Case.
6. What is Punctuation? Give rules for principal marks of Punctuation.
7-10. Write a composition of about 150 words and show therein that you understand the practical use of the rules of grammar.

ARITHMETIC
(Time, 1 1/2 hours)

1. Name and define the Fundamental Rules of Arithmetic.
2. A wagon box is 2 ft. deep, 10 feet long, and 3 ft. wide. How many bushels of wheat will it hold?
3. If a load of wheat weighs 3,942 lbs., what is it worth at 50 cts. per bu., deducting 1,050 lbs. for tare?
4. District No. 33 has a valuation of $35,000. What is the necessary levy to carry on a school seven months at $50 per month, and have $104 for incidentals?
5. Find cost of 6,720 lbs. coal at $6.00 per ton.
6. Find the interest of $512.60 for 8 months and 18 days at 7 per cent.
7. What is the cost of 40 boards 12 inches wide and 16 ft. long at $20 per m.?
8. Find bank discount on $300 for 90 days (no grace) at 10 per cent.
9. What is the cost of a square farm at $15 per acre, the distance around which is 640 rods?
10. Write a Bank Check, a Promissory Note, and a Receipt.

U.S. HISTORY
(Time, 45 minutes)

1. Give the epochs into which U.S. History is divided.
2. Give an account of the discovery of America by Columbus.
3. Relate the causes and results of the Revolutionary War.
4. Show the territorial growth of the United States.
5. Tell what you can of the history of Kansas.
6. Describe three of the most prominent battles of the Rebellion.
7. Who were the following: Morse, Whitney, Fulton, Bell, Lincoln, Penn and Howe?
8. Name events connected with the following dates: 1607, 1620, 1800, 1849 and 1865.

ORTHOGRAPHY
(Time, 1 1/2 hours)

1. What is meant by the following: Alphabet, phonetic, orthography, etymology, syllabication?
2. What are elementary sounds? How classified?
3. What are the following, and give examples of each: Trigraph, subvocals, diphthong, cognate letters, linguals?
4. Give four substitutes for caret "u".
5. Give two rules for spelling words with final "e." Name two exceptions under each rule.
6. Give two uses of silent letters in spelling. Illustrate each.
7. Define the following prefixes and use in connection with a word: Di, dis, mis, pre, semi, post, non, inter, mono, super.
8. Mark diacritically and divide into syllables the following, and name the sign that indicates the sound: Card, ball, mercy, sir, odd, cell, rise, blood, fare, last.
9. Use the following correctly in sentences: Cite, site, sight, fane, fain, feign, vane, vain, vein, raze, raise, rays.
10. Write 10 words frequently mispronounced and indicate pronunciation by use of diacritical marks and by syllabication.

GEOGRAPHY
(Time, one hour)

1. What is climate? Upon what does climate depend?
2. How do you account for the extremes of climate in Kansas?
3. Of what use are rivers? Of what use is the ocean?
4. Describe the mountains of N.A.
5. Name and describe the following: Moarovia, Odessa, Denver, Manitoba, Hecla, Yukon, St. Helena, Juan Fernandez, Aspinwall, and Orinoco.
6. Name and locate the principal trade centers of the U.S.
7. Name all the republics of Europe and give capital of each.
8. Why is the Atlantic Coast colder than the Pacific in same latitude?
9. Describe the process by which the water of the ocean returns to the sources of rivers.
10. Describe the movements of the earth. Give inclination of the earth.

PHYSIOLOGY
(Time, 45 minutes)

1. Where are the saliva, gastric juice, and bile secreted? What is the use of each in digestion?
2. How does nutrition reach the circulation?
3. What is the function of the liver? Of the kidneys?
4. How would you stop the flow of blood from an artery in case of laceration?
5. Give some general directions that you think would be beneficial to preserve the human body in a state of health.

RAYMOND C. SIMON

Crow Chief Plenty Coups; visionary, warrior, and
leader of the Mountain Crows of the Crow
Nation and friend to Ray's Great-grandmother, Mary
Almira George Wheeler, and his Mother, Etta May
Bruce Simon

Chief Plenty Coups gifted Ray's mother, Etta Bruce,
with a pair of Crow tribal war beaded moccasin
covers in 1912

Crow Nation Chief Plenty Coups, tribal
representative at the funeral of the World War I
Unknown Soldier, Arlington National Cemetery in
November of 1921

Gene Speck, Western artist, original oil, Crow Camp

Gene Speck, Western Artist, original oil

Gene Speck, Western Artist, original oil

2

GROWING UP

The Great Depression, which spanned 3-1/2 years from August 1929-March 1933, impacted my family, as it did everyone in that era. The 31st President of the United States, Herbert Hoover, experienced the hardship of this devastating era essentially his entire presidency. Some causes blamed for setting off and contributing to the Great Depression: the stock market crash of 1929; collapse of world trade; government policies (expanding major sections of government); panic and closures in the banking system; and collapse of the money supply.

My father worked four jobs during this time, during and after our Country's recovery, for which he was very grateful. Besides working at the Hennessy Lumber Milling Company, he ran the Grizzly Service Station, was City Treasurer, and drove an oil truck for two different cities to maintain the service stations. He was on the Conrad

School board also. I don't know if he received a stipend for his elected service.

We never suffered; we made stuff on our own, and you can be sure we could get pretty creative. We were poor at this time but I never knew it.

At the Hennessy Lumber Milling Company my dad loaded and unloaded lumber at the Northern Pacific Railway site. I remember railroad stations back then had water towers which held thousands of gallons of water. Steam locomotives needed to consistently stop to fill their water tanks, as the engine would run on steam power, so the trains always interrupted their journey for this purpose at our station. Some stations had a track pan which allowed a steam locomotive to fill its tanks without stopping which consisted of a long trench of water sitting between the rails. When the train rode over this channel, a scoop fed water into a pipe which fed the locomotive tanks, also called the locomotive tender.

It was common for men who were looking for work to hop the trains from Back East to the West, hitching a ride on the top of railroad cars or jumping into an empty freight railroad car. Whenever the train stopped, a lot of the men would take the opportunity to get off the train to get food and water and look for work. Oftentimes they would ask if a local could give them something to eat, or trade work for food. They were called hobos, and in that day and time they were usually decent, hardworking men looking for a better life, and townspeople were happy to help them.

One day in particular this man jumped off the train and

walked into my dad's office and asked if he had any food. "Yes, you may come home with me and have lunch," my dad told him. So he walked in with my dad, and since my mother was used to this kind of occurrence, she simply set another place at the table.

I was only about three years old but I distinctly remember him, probably because he didn't look like any of the other drifters my dad had brought home to feed. He was dressed very nicely in tan work pants, a dark brown leather jacket, and was quite good looking. He also seemed to be keeping an eye on me which made me stare at him even more.

Even stranger was his behavior. He never talked. He didn't speak or answer questions. He simply ate his lunch, politely thanked us, and left.

Well, our local sheriff came to visit us a few hours later. Sheriff Munson knew my dad worked at the railroad and he brought a telegraph message and photo, and asked, "Have you seen this guy?"

"Yes, we just gave him lunch," my dad answered.

"Which way did he go?" The sheriff asked.

My dad told him, "I don't know but the train was going west."

The man was Pretty Boy Floyd, and my mom was flabbergasted that we had served lunch to a bank robber and killer in our home. We were also impressed, though, that he seemed such a gentleman, and we could see how he'd be a popular figure in spite of his criminal history.

Floyd was hunted and finally shot down by a team of local police and FBI agents led by Melvin Purvis on

October 22, 1934 in a corn field in East Liverpool, Ohio. However much a gangster Pretty Boy Floyd was thought to be, he had charmed a nation. Over 20,000 people attended his funeral, and 20 states were represented by motorcars.

I have a lot of fond memories of my family and my life in Conrad as a young boy. When I look back, it seems to me that I had an interest in just about everything that happened, and I learned so much from my mother, father, brothers and sisters.

The six of us Simon children were all born in about a 12-year span. We figured that our mother gave birth nearly every one and a half years. Mary started the trend in 1921. Her birth was followed by Dave, Jim, Jeanne, myself, and baby brother Bill.

Our home in Conrad was mid-sized and very nice looking with white pillars and a large porch across the front. We had a beautiful yard. My mother loved to raise flowers and planted all different kinds of bushes and trees.

The house had a kitchen, large living room, formal dining room, two bedrooms, one bathroom, a large concrete basement and a root cellar. Our bathroom had a tub, basin, and toilet. In that era, some homes still utilized outhouses, and we considered ourselves very fortunate.

It's hard to imagine eight people sharing one bathroom in the house, but that seemed pretty normal to us and it somehow worked out as we learned to take turns for everything. I remember Saturday night was my turn to bathe with my little brother Bill, I suppose because we were the youngest. The other kids had their own schedules for bathing once a week.

My parents had an Atwater Kent radio in their living room. We'd all gather around and listen to The Lone Ranger, Flash Gordon, and I Love a Mystery. My family didn't have a TV until 1950.

The first TV I remember seeing was when I went into the Air Force, where they had a color TV in the barracks day room. Our whole group would gather there and watch TV on Sunday nights, especially Lawrence Welk, the Perry Como Show, and I Love Lucy. Other popular shows during that time were The Adventures of Superman, The Lone Ranger, Sky King, Father Knows Best, The Cisco Kid, Air Force, The Honeymooners, and Your Show of Shows with comedians Imogene Coca and Sid Caesar.

While my parents' bedroom was upstairs where my two sisters Mary and Jeanne also shared a room, my brothers Dave, Jim, Bill and I were deigned to sleep in the basement which contained a new large Holland gas fed furnace for the home.

Down in that basement my father also had a large wooden countertop which he used to cut meat. He had all the knives and appropriate implements and would buy a butchered pig and half a beef in huge slabs from a local farmer/butcher who raised cattle and hogs. My dad would cut the slabs into sizable pieces, wrap them in butcher paper and store them in the root cellar portion of the basement which was dug down about two feet lower than the rest of the basement.

My dad built that root cellar. They used a team of

horses pulling a box scraper blade — which is made for grading and scraping — to dig the basement and cellar. The cellar had a wooden floor and door, and no windows, and our light for that room was one lone lightbulb that hung down from the ceiling in the center of that space.

There were shelves on the dirt walls for canned and dry goods and the meat, and it stayed very cold all year 'round. There was a wooden box maybe two feet wide by six feet long at the far end of the cellar. Once a week the Ice Man would come and dump a block of ice into that box, just during the summer.

In those days we had to be extremely self-sufficient living in a remote town like Conrad. Next door to us was a vacant lot, and every year my parents would plant it full of all kinds of vegetables; anything that they could. My mother would can everything that was picked and probably had 150 cans of beets, corn, carrots, and peas, plus sacks of potatoes that we'd grown, all stored down in the root cellar each year.

It was great fun during the summer making homemade root beer. We had our own syrup we could use, and we would add various elements to it, stir it up in a big tub, and pour it into various bottles that my father had collected.

We all had daily chores. We had to, with that many kids. You can imagine Mother taking care of six children and having to direct them into specific jobs so that she did not work herself to death.

I was probably five years old, washing dishes standing on a stool. My little brother Bill would dry. As we got a little older, our job was to pick up the dishes from the table and put them in the kitchen so that two of my sisters could wash and dry them.

My favorite job was to polish all the silver and shine everything in the house. Shining items was my specialty – I loved polishing and my mother allowed me to have that job permanently. I still enjoy that same thing today and my wife Joan often takes advantage of this cathartic exercise and has me polish the silver from time to time.

We also had some specific summertime chores. One of my brother Dave's jobs – during spring cleaning – was to take the rugs outside and hang them on the clothesline so he could whip the dust and dirt out of the house carpets. I remember the distinct whirring sound it made as he found his rhythm punching the rugs on and on.

Also in the summertime Jim had to pick dandelions out of the front and back yard, the leaves of which our mother put into salads and soups. While numerous people consider the dandelion a weed, they are also seen as herbs, and many use the stem, leaves, flower and roots for medicinal purposes.

My father had a sister who also lived in Conrad who I was very close to. Aunt Blanche and Uncle Fred Webster would invite me to stay overnight with them pretty often when I was quite young, just a couple of years old, and I like to think it was because I was their favorite – of course! She always liked to tell me that I'd go to sleep in her arms and I'd twirl her hair as I guess I found it soothing. She'd laugh that by the time I fell asleep her hair was a mess. Thinking back to that time, it's possible they were just taking me off my mother's hands so she could recover from childbirth and focus on newborn baby Bill.

Eventually Fred and Blanche moved to Cut Bank, Montana, about 60 miles away when he went to work as an engineer for the Union Oil Company. One day there was a fire and explosion at one of the plants where they were converting the oil to gas. Fred was outside and knew some of his workers were trapped so he ran inside to rescue them. He was burned terribly, and it was obvious he was not going to make it.

Blanche called my dad and said, "Fred wants to see you, and you need to come right away." My parents took off straight away. Fred was in horrible pain, and my dad told us that when he first came into the room, Fred begged him, "Please, put a pillow over my head," and my dad told him, "I'm sorry Fred, I can't do that." About two or three hours later he did die. My father didn't tell us that story until quite a long time after the funeral.

I had two good friends as a young boy. One was Bunny Norley, whose father was the Mayor of Conrad and also had a men's shop in the downtown area. The other was Tony Bannister, whose father was a physician, as was his mother. They were doctors of osteopathy and were among the wealthiest people in Conrad. They both had come from Canada and lived in a stunning two-story home, which was beautifully decorated with English-style furniture.

The four seasons: fall, winter, spring, and summer, were very distinct in Conrad. I recall that many winters were extremely severe -- temperatures many times dropped way below zero. One time when it was 32° below, everything in the city stopped. It was always an excitement to wake up in the morning and find snow covering all of your windows six feet high and stacked around our house. Walking to school was a thrill — to cover your face entirely with a scarf so that your nose didn't freeze offered the opportunity to pretend you were a bank robber or masked champion. The long walks in the snow presented uncountable prospects to use my youthful imagination.

Fall was a beautiful time of the year in Conrad, and our city was landscaped with many deciduous trees. The leaves changed color before they would fall to cover the ground to create a delightful organic blanket; specifically the many maple trees with leaves that changed from green to a stunning red and orange and yellow.

Spring was a magnificent period when the snow began to melt and small flowers would pop up everywhere along the sidewalks and in our backyard. Whether it was snow in the winter or a sunny spring day, the walk was always enjoyable.

Conrad had a grade school, full complement kindergarten through eighth grade, and a high school. I remember a big staircase at Conrad High School that seemed very impressive to my young mind. Our mascots were the Cowboys and Cowgirls and our classrooms had blackboards which originally were made of black slate.

The first blackboard was created in 1801 by a geography teacher in Scotland. The slate blackboard was used in schools until the 1960s when they were replaced by the greenboard (still called a "blackboard," however), a steel plate coated with a porcelain based enamel, which was replaced more recently by digital whiteboards. I would imagine there are still schools that use blackboards and chalk.

We never packed our lunch; we'd walk home to eat. Usually lunch consisted of a slice of bread with butter and a little sugar sprinkled on it, and milk. Sometimes my mother would heat up the milk with butter and if the bread was dry, we'd dip it in the milk or she'd put pieces of the bread in the warm milk and serve it that way.

I absolutely loved school, especially the 1st grade mostly because I had fallen in love with my first-grade teacher, Miss Pichare. She was the most beautiful woman I had ever seen and I could hardly wait to go to school each day. In fact I always sat in the first row so she couldn't miss me. At some point she met a handsome teacher who taught high school and when she married him, they moved to Great Falls, Montana. My first heartbreak.

We had a principal in grade school, Mr. Brady who had six kids of his own. Mr. Brady was one of the meanest adults I've ever known. Unlike my crush on Miss Pichare, Mr. Brady left no illusion as to his relationship with students. His preferred method with the younger students was to purposefully strike their fingers with a ruler. The eighth-grade boys were whipped with a hose that Mr. Brady actually kept hanging on the wall in his office.

One day Miss Pichare had a substitute fill in for her, a Mrs. Armstrong, who thought I was talking too much so she called the principal who was very happy to walk down to our classroom to take care of business. Mr. Brady told me to put my fingers on my desk and he smacked them quite severely with his ruler. Remember, I was in the first grade and only six years old.

I dashed out of the school room and ran home but I was embarrassed to go into the house. I hid outside crying in shame until my mother came out looking for me, and immediately she called my dad who came right home. Unfortunately for Mr. Brady it turned out that my dad was a member of the school board. He interviewed all of the 8th grade boys as well as other grades, and did not hesitate to fire Mr. Brady.

W e lived only ninety miles from Glacier National Park, and many times during the summer we would travel to the park and spend a weekend living in a tent, fishing or playing in Lake McDonald. I loved the picnic dinners my mother prepared on those outings — potato salad and cold chicken — and we would also eat the trout my father and brothers would catch.

We'd pick chokecherries and come home with tons of them. Mother would hang them in bags in the basement letting the juice drip into the pan, and then she would either make jam and jelly, or syrup, and we would have that all during the winter.

My mother had great hopes for me and said that she named me Raymond after the silent movie star Ramon Navarro. A Mexican-American silent movie star, Navarro had become a top box office attraction and leading man in the 1920s and '30s.

Mother could sing very beautifully and taught me to sing, and we soon found out that even though I couldn't read music, I could hear a song once and sing it flawlessly. I had an innate ability for music, so my parents took advantage of that and entered me in a singing contest in Conrad. I won that contest singing "You Must Have Been a Beautiful Baby." I was five years old and it was my favorite song. I can still hear it – I'll never forget that song.

When I was seven years old it was the two eldest ring-leaders— my siblings Mary and Dave already out of high school — who took their little brother to a saloon called

Little America and put me on top of the bar so patrons could see me while I serenaded my audience. I would sing for about half an hour every song I knew – especially my favorites like *Goody Goody*, and *You Must Have Been A Beautiful Baby*. You can Google "You Must Have Been a Beautiful Baby" and "Frankie Lyman Goody Goody" if you want to hear for yourself why they were such popular songs and so fun to sing. Johnny Mercer wrote the lyrics for both songs. Dave and Mary, of course, for all my trouble got a beer which they were undoubtedly quite happy about.

———

I only got to meet my paternal grandparents George and Mary Simon once, when we drove to Bridger, Montana for the Jim Bridger celebration. It's hard to believe we made the five-six hour drive with the whole family packed into our big old-fashioned REO automobile, but that's what we did.

Ransom Eli Olds had founded the Oldsmobile Motor Works Company (originally the Olds Motor Works) in 1897, and when he left Oldsmobile and started another automobile company in 1904 he used his initials R.E.O. because he could no longer use his name "Olds" in the designation of the new company. Into the 1990s, REO trucks were still being produced.

Since 1838 the Jim Bridger celebration, also called the Fort Bridger Mountain Man Rendezvous, annually commemorates fur trappers, traders, and mountain men who followed Lewis and Clark in the early western expeditions, and especially Jim Bridger who mediated between Indigenous Americans and settlers heading West and told colorful stories of his experiences. The celebration is still observed to this day.

We stayed in my grandparents' home, which had a rather large, swift canal in front of it that ran through the center of town. Late on the afternoon of our arrival, my cousin Jack Harrington and I went down to play and throw rocks into the canal. We both fell in and struggled to get out but couldn't because of the steep concrete sides of the canal. We began screaming and yelling for help.

As luck would have it — I call it divine intervention — a man standing on a walking bridge a few yards down from us managed to get over to the side and grabbed both of us by the collar. Otherwise, I think we would've drowned. This was the first appearance of my guardian angel or angels that I can recall. When we were safely out of the water, the man disappeared, and we never saw him again.

Jack and I, looking and feeling like drowned rats, hugged each other like there was no tomorrow. We tried to put on a brave face but cried most of the way home. When my cousin and I walked into the house, we burst into tears trying to tell everyone what had happened.

Grandfather was upset that we'd been so careless, but Grandmother tried to soothe our frayed nerves and got us into some dry clothes; matching sailor suits as I recall. She then proceeded to feed us until eventually we could calmly tell them exactly what had happened. Of course my mother and grandmother felt it was a miraculous turn of events; angels interfering to stop a disastrous occurrence.

The very next day after our arrival Grandpa George asked me if I wanted to go to the ice cream store. I, of course, said yes, and stood in the doorway watching him get ready to go. I was quite surprised to see how short he was, whereas my Grandmother Mary was a rather tall and large woman. I think Grandpa was around five feet six, with a great big handlebar mustache. After he got his trousers on, I watched him put on a shirt, and over the shirt he donned shoulder holsters into which he placed pearl-handled pistols snug to his sides, one under each arm. He then put his jacket on.

I asked him, "Grandpa, why are you wearing those guns?"

He exclaimed, "You never know when you may need them in this town, especially since I'm also going to the bar for a drink."

I don't think I will ever forget that sight.

After some time, I asked my father why Grandfather was drinking at noon, and my father said, "When your grandpa was in the mines working and digging coal, they would stop every morning for a bucket of whiskey. Every single miner would drink a bucket of whiskey. They did so because it's disastrous to work underground with only a candle in your hat."

One thing that always stuck with me was the amount of pestilence we had in those early years in Conrad. I don't think people today really realize or would remember that there used to be great hordes of grasshoppers up north that would invade the wheatlands all around Conrad.

I remember my father having to go with a team of men with horses and shovels and carve out trenches throughout the wheat fields and fill them with oil, then set them on fire and chase the grasshoppers in. The grasshoppers were so thick they would hang on to the screens outside our house, and my mother and father used to have to go out with brooms in the morning and sweep them off the screens and spray them with DDT (dichloro-diphenyl-trichloroethane). DDT was developed in 1874, but it wasn't until 1939 it was discovered to work as an insecticide. Before it was banned for use in the United States, it was used to fight malaria, typhus, and later as a very effective pesticide.

A couple of years later, there was a whole infestation of beetles — beautiful colored beetles that covered the side of our house to such an extent you couldn't tell we even had a house there. Again, we had to go to dreadful kinds of treatment.

I 've always marveled at how the town of Conrad could have had so many areas of business and commerce. Conrad had a bank that was run by Mr. Kumpf who lived behind us, and boasted a Chevrolet, Buick, Ford, and of course, Allis-Chalmers dealer. We had many specialty shops, ladies' shops, and Arnott's General Store, as well as a full-fledged creamery that produced wonderful bottles of milk and they made ice cream all year long. There were also two drugstores, and the Conrad Hotel.

Arnott's was a full grocery store where we could buy everything we needed, including meat. The biggest thrill for me though, when Mother would take me along, was to buy a pack of Wrigley's spearmint gum. It cost me all of 5¢ and you can believe it was quite a treat.

We had a hospital called St. Mary's that was run by Catholic nuns. There were also a good number of doctors. Dr. Patterson was a general physician and surgeon. The two Powers brothers were physicians and surgeons. There was Dr. DuBois and the two Drs. Bannister. I used to visit most of these people, who were in my neighborhood, as a little boy pulling a wagon and trying to sell the various housewares — old toothbrushes and any old thing my mother threw away. In most cases, I was able to get a couple pennies for some of these things.

There were many times when my family had to go looking for me. Several times, they even had the sheriff trying to find me. One time, they found me in a new Chevrolet sedan in the showroom of the Chevrolet dealer with the radio on, listening to music. I've loved music my whole life. I remember sitting on our front porch hearing Western music playing, coming from downtown, probably the Conrad Hotel. When I asked my dad if he would take me down there, of course he did.

My favorite Western singers came into town on a flat wagon with an orchestra and played music for the folks of Conrad. I specifically remember one guy who played the guitar named Powder River Jack with his wife Kitty Lee. They would sing cowboy songs at rodeos and fairs, and he also played in Buffalo Bill Cody's Wild West Show. Some of his songs that come to mind are Red River Valley, Song of San Marcos, Across the Great Divide, and The Cody Stampede.

Simon Family. Top Row, L-R: Jim, Father Dave Sr., Dave, Jr.
Bottom Row, L-R: Ray and Bill (1938)

Simon Family. Top Row, L-R: Dave, Jr, Bill, Jim, Ray. Bottom
Row, L-R: Father Dave Sr., Jeanne, Mary, Mother Etta (1946)

L-R: Mrs. Maysel Anderson, 10-year-old Joan
Pedego, Jean Smith, and Joan's dance instructor
— Bette Belle Anderson Smith (1946)

3

THE WAR YEARS

I was playing in the front yard on a Sunday morning when my friend Bunny ran over with his brother Lou to see my brother Jim, shouting, "The Japanese are bombing Pearl Harbor! We are going to war!" The date was December 7, 1941.

I was totally fascinated by the war. My brother Jim was drafted and went into the Army Air Corps as a navigator in a B-17 squadron in the United Kingdom. Bunny's brother Lou Norley also went to England and joined the Royal Air Force (RAF) as a Spitfire pilot. He became a legend shooting down Messerschmitts, the WWII German fighter aircraft named after its chief designer, Willy Messerschmitt. They nicknamed Lou "Red Dog Norley," and at one point he was named Commanding Officer of the 335th Fighter Squadron and was eventually awarded the Distinguished Flying Cross and the Air Medal with 13 Oak Leaf Clusters.

During World War II our neighbor in Conrad, Sverre Askevold, a general contractor who was originally from Fkordane, Norway, asked my father to join him in bidding on government contracts which were plentiful during that time.

My father's mathematics skills continued to lead him to better opportunities and he became the treasurer of a large construction company. We moved from Conrad to Great Falls, Montana, where the air base was being expanded to accommodate the transfer of P-41 fighter planes to Russia.

My sister Mary met a pilot, Herbert Bronson, who was in Great Falls for training and was going to transfer to Africa, flying a B-24 bomber. I was totally thrilled with him as he was a handsome man from Texas, a captain wearing beautiful pink and drab green uniforms. To me, he was a hero. He never did return to California or Montana, and no one ever knew what happened to him in World War II. My sister was devastated. He had given her an engagement ring before leaving.

Later, we moved to Portland, Oregon for another contract, this time with Kaiser Shipyards where they were building Liberty Ships at the rate of one per day. Henry J. Kaiser was a mastermind who helped win the war by building these ships. They transported military goods and men around the world.

While we were living in Portland, my mother read in

the newspaper that a Broadway producer and director by the name of Donald Marie was coming to Portland to teach dramatic arts at the Portland Civic Theater and would be training a number of people in summer stock. My mother wanted me to attend this school, and I did. I was 12 years old and rode the trolley down to central Portland and attended these lessons in projection, pronunciation, theater protocol, and anything related to acting. I was in a number of productions, and on one occasion tried out for a summer stock play which entailed the actors travel to all of the military bases on the West Coast, journeying away from home by train or bus for one month.

I got the part and learned that I was to be accompanied by a retired schoolteacher as my guardian. I then found out that the lead in the play was none other than the movie star, Ethel Barrymore. The play was called *The Tree and I* and we played all of the military basis on the West Coast.

She would have been around 64 years old around that time. Everyone knew about the famous family of Barrymore radio, stage, and screen actors, including the legendary Lionel (1878-1954), John (1882-1942), and of course present-day Drew Barrymore. In 1928, the celebrated actress had opened a theatre in New York named for her.

After our stay in Portland, it was time to move on to Merced, California, where my father had a contract to expand Castle Air Force Base. He also bought a bowling alley as an investment, and I spent a great deal of time there bowling and also playing pool. It was right in the middle of World War II, and we as a family had to deal with shortages, including gasoline and food items like butter, sugar, coffee, meat, canned fish, cheese and canned milk, just like everyone else at that time.

It was easy for me to get a job at age fourteen as a busboy in the Hotel Tioga as well as a dishwasher. All of the young men had gone off to war. I actually had two jobs: one was in the hotel and the other was melting lead for linotype at the Merced SunStar newspaper office for Mr. Lesher. The linotype (line-o-type) machine composed complete lines of words into single strips of metal instead of individual characters.

One of my more interesting experiences occurred when Mr. Lesher asked me to substitute for the newspaper delivery boy who was sick. One of the stops on my delivery was at a two-story white house on West Seventh Street. Little did I know what went on in that house. The lady who always met me at the door was named Mabel, and she was a middle-aged woman, rather rotund and very pleasant. She would ask me if I could go to the drugstore to pick up prescriptions for her, and she would give me a five-dollar bill. That, frankly, was a fortune.

One day when I pulled up on my bicycle, she said,

"Would you like some pie? I just made a banana cream pie."

Of course I said yes. When I went into the kitchen, much to my surprise, I saw a long table with about twelve of the most beautiful women I'd ever seen in my life. All of them had the same platinum blonde hair. They were eating lunch and altogether gave me big smiles as I walked in.

I sat next to a particularly attractive gal who looked at me and said, "How old are you, Ray?"

I said, "I am fourteen going on fifteen."

She said, "That's just the right age. When we're done with lunch, I intend to take you upstairs and make a real man out of you — for free!"

I did not know what she meant, but Miss Mabel did! She reached over and swatted the girl on her head and said, "You leave him alone! Don't you ever say anything like that to him again."

On Mother's Day, I went by the florist shop and saw a beautiful rose in a glass bowl. It was not cheap — it was about five dollars. I had saved a lot of money from all of my jobs. I took it home to my mother and she was extremely happy with it.

Then she asked me how I could afford this, and I told her about Miss Mabel and about my jobs. She said, "Who is this Miss Mabel?"

I told her Miss Mabel lived in a large two-story house, and how she always had a lot of girls at a long table for lunch. My mother took one look at me and then looked at my father and said, "You know who that is, don't you?"

My father looked rather strangely at my mother and

then said, "You are to quit delivering papers right now and never go back there again."

Later on, I relayed this story to my friends. My all-knowing, very mature friend Billy Riker was an older boy of about sixteen, and he knew just about everything there was to know about anybody and anything. All the boys sought him out for advice, and believe me, he was full of information. When I told him of my experience with Mabel, he actually knew who she was. He said, "Don't you know what that place is? Those girls are for the air base entertainment."

Working at the Merced SunStar and melting lead helped me catch up with all the news about the war. I knew every single battle that went on, especially the bombings over Germany, and that my brother was flying as a navigator in a B-17.

One day while in school in the eighth grade, I can recall our teacher coming in and saying, "President Roosevelt has died, and we are terminating school for several days of mourning." Losing the president in the middle of a war was very traumatic for most Americans, and the sadness was widespread.

While in Merced when I was about 13 or 14 years old, I had a good friend named George Jensen. George was with me almost constantly. We were very close; best friends really.

One Sunday, George and I decided to ride our bikes to Lake Merced. When we arrived, the sun was out, and it was a rather pleasant day. We knew a girl named Sheila Flanigan who had a wonderful little dinghy with a sail at the lake and she had just docked it. We asked her if we could borrow it and try to sail it. She said okay, so we got in the boat and sailed it out into the center of Lake Merced, which is quite large.

Suddenly, a huge and terrific storm set in. It was raining and blowing so hard that it blew us over into the water, and the boat began to sink. It would've been several miles for us to swim ashore and we couldn't possibly do it, so we hung onto the boat all the while fearing that it would sink. We were at the point of almost letting go when I looked at him across the bottom of the boat and said, "I think we're going to drown, George. Let's try to swim," even though I knew it was of no use.

Just then, we heard the sound of a powerboat. Out of the fog and rain and wind came a man in a medium-sized motorboat who said, "I saw you boys go down, and decided I better come out and help." Again, to me, it was a display of divine intervention by our angels. I went home that afternoon and told my parents what had happened. It was such a frightening event and I was crying so hard I could hardly get the story out; I just couldn't seem to stop.

My mother insisted, "You were lucky Ray, you and your friend George. Your guardian angel brought that man from shore during the storm to save your life."

The struggle George and I experienced trying to survive made us realize that there was no escape for us, that we were doomed and this is what it must be like to feel completely helpless. It was so terrifying hanging onto that little overturned boat, struggling to stay alive and praying to God that whatever deal we had to make with Him to please listen to us and save us.

That experience changed my life and George's irrevocably. I believe George learned how to swim soon after, and in his adult life he became a captain in the Navy.

U p to this point the Lutheran church had been a huge influence on me, having been baptized there and being involved with that denomination exclusively. However, when we moved to Merced, we found there was no Lutheran church. Fortunately, near where we lived was a Baptist Church. It really did not matter to me which church I attended, as long as I could be present to enjoy the speaking and singing.

It was at the Baptist church that they announced one day a traveling minister named Johnny Lavender would be presenting a week's worth of sermons on healing. At the first sermon I was blown away listening to this young minister who was the most appealing and thrilling speaker

I had ever heard in my life. I was absolutely drawn into his sermon which was centered around God and His helpers, the angels, including divine interventions as they relate to healing.

He was such an inspirational speaker I could hardly wait to go home and tell my mother about his speech. I looked forward to the next six days being in his presence and finding out what he had in store for us, and it was not disappointing. I was so thrilled with his approach exposing me to this knowledge of God's helpers, the angels that I told my parents I thought I should become a minister, if only I could present myself the way this man did.

Johnny Lavender's talks on healing were so profound, so soul touching and inspirational that I don't have the words to describe how it truly filled me with God's light, and hope, and change.

———

Shortly thereafter, we decided — that is, my dad decided — to move back to Missoula, as he had several contracts to fulfill, one being the construction of Hungry Horse Dam near Kalispell, Montana, and in Arco, Idaho an atomic energy plant where the first atomic submarine was to be built.

In the Montana oil rush of 1900-1901 two freight horses wandered away and weren't found for about a month, starving and stuck in snow. They were nurtured back to health and became quite celebrated, thus the name Hungry

Horse Dam. It's one of the United States' biggest concrete arch dams at 564 feet high, and it boasts the highest morning glory spillway in the world at 490 feet.

In Arco, Idaho tourists are welcomed for self-guided tours of the atomic energy plant, and they boast an "Atomic Days" celebration held each summer.

High school was a lot of fun, at least for me. Fishing was an extracurricular activity that everyone engaged in. Anyone worth their salt could fly-fish. Fish Creek State Park, Montana had the best fishing streams in the world. You could catch twelve- to eighteen-inch trout all the time. There were beaver dams along many of the streams, and those were always full of fish. If you saw the movie *A River Runs Through It*, those scenes were filmed in Montana around all the streams I fished, from the Bitterroot to Flathead Lake.

I began tying my own flies and experimenting with them. The best time of year was when the season opened in March. One year, salmonflies were in vogue. The salmonfly is large, which makes them ideal bait for trout fishing with a rod and line, and I got pretty good at making them. They were very realistic looking. At that time of my life I thought school wasn't for me and I really wasn't much of a student. I seemed to be more interested in running around with my friends, fishing, going to the movies, and singing.

The Northern Pacific Railway Company was chartered by Congress in 1864 to build a line from Lake Superior (Carlton, Minnesota) westward to a port on the Pacific Coast. It was built to Helena in Montana Territory, where it was connected with the Oregon Railway to Seattle in Washington Territory in 1883.

My best friend was Tom Rollins. Alan Tweto and Dave Hurtt were other friends of mine. Every summer, Alan and Tom worked with me on the Northern Pacific Railroad. We got a job on the bridge-building crew by faking our age; you had to be eighteen, and we were only fifteen. Tom's mother worked for the city or county clerk's office, and she was able to give us blank birth certificates, which we took to my dad's office and typed out, declaring we were eighteen.

We worked on that bridge-building crew for the first year in the summer and in the second and third year of high school or fourth year, we were able to get on the paint crew painting railroad traffic signals, some railroad homes, and anything else that needed constant maintenance. We were fed by the wife of the straw boss — assistant to the foreman — and stayed in one of the railroad cars. I believe we only paid twenty-five cents for three meals a day and our boxcar room, which sat along the siding on the railroad.

My singing job in high school came during a cantata which is a composition for vocal soloists, or chorus and orchestra. When the director discovered that I had a voice, he decided to put me in an operetta called *Trial by Jury*. I was to play the part of the defending attorney. It was called the biggest, most successful performance by a group of people of a Gilbert and Sullivan operetta ever presented, and I became quite popular.

My father and I used to fish a lot. On one occasion, we drove to a spot on a hill above the Clark Fork River. This river is unusual in that it flows in an irregular course north and northwest for about 360 miles – something I didn't realize as a young boy who was only interested in enjoying the cool water, spending this peaceful time with my dad, and catching as many rainbow, brown or cutthroat trout as we could. You'll find some of the very best dry fly fishing in the lower Clark Fork because of its plentiful hatches.

We had to climb down the hill and get into the river along a high granite wall with swift water. We came to the other side and it smoothed out into a huge beautiful green valley with a lot of beaver dams.

We could wade to the beaver dams and started catching trout as fast as you could pull your line in. We probably caught twenty-eight fish between us. Suddenly, my dad put his finger to his lips, signaling "Shush!" He pointed downstream where there were five black bears crossing in front of us — one huge male and a female with three baby bears. Thank God they couldn't smell us because we were downwind. They finally moved on, and we breathed a sigh of relief.

However, upon deciding to return to our starting point,

I heard sounds to my left coming from the riverbank, and when I looked, I saw a group of three bobcats watching us and following us upstream. Now, bobcats are small but mean. We made a decision to throw fish every few yards until we could get out of sight, and it worked — they left us alone.

4

IN THE AIR FORCE

When I graduated, I decided to enter the University of Montana for a pre dental major, which I did not follow through on. I was not a good student there either. I joined a fraternity called Sigma Nu and barely made it in with my grades. While I was in Sigma Nu, the Korean War broke out, and I had a draft card with a number that was going to be called out very shortly.

I decided I didn't want to go into the Army so before they would draft me, I joined the Air Force as did about thirty of my friends in the fraternity, particularly Jerry Stoick and Fred Deschamps. Fifteen of us boarded a train in Missoula to head for Lackland Air Force Base, which was the entry into the Air Force. We traveled by train all the way to San Antonio, Texas, and upon arrival, we realized that 14,000 other recruits were already there. There were no beds, so we slept in the ballpark at the base and tried to stay warm wrapped in newspaper. We had little or no chance to have food, so those of us who had money would go to the PX— the Post Exchange, which is the Air Force retail store — and buy candy bars to live on. We lived this way for approximately a week and a half.

A general arrived from Washington, D.C. to take the matter in hand. We went through basic training for eight weeks and then took a test to determine which division of the Air Force we were going to be assigned. I was chosen as an engine and aircraft specialist in aviation mechanics and transferred to Chanute Air Force Base in Champaign County, Illinois where I attended the School of Engines, Aircraft, and Mechanics for one solid year.

For the next six months while still at Chanute, I went through the U.S. Air Force Flight Engineer School, then was assigned to the Fifth Air Force 99th bomb squadron at Travis Air Force Base in California. That was where we learned how to load and unload an atomic bomb – the A-bomb.

In San Antonio, Texas I trained to become a flight engineer on the B-29 Superfortress. At this juncture in my life, I became Staff Sergeant Simon of the United States Air Force during the Korean Conflict, and served in the Strategic Air Command as a B-29 flight engineer.

The bombs were massive, and to load them onto the aircraft we had to use loading pits. The bomber aircraft, with its bomb bay doors open, would be towed directly over the pit. The bomb was then pulled onto the hydraulic mount and winched very carefully into the belly of the airplane.

The B-29 was developed in 1940, replacing the B-17 and

B-24. This new Superbomber was on the cutting edge with many improvements including remote-controlled machine gun turrets, pressurized cabin, and central fire-control system which, as you can imagine, was immense progress.

Our whole squadron, including 12 Superbombers, were to leave Travis Air Force Base for Guam in the Solomon Islands of the South Pacific. Our crew included an airplane commander, copilot, bombardier-DR navigator, navigator-radar specialist, flight engineer, radio operator, radar gunner, electrical specialist gunner, air mechanic gunner, central fire control specialist, and tail gunner.

Our pilot, Captain Paul Aldhizer, was a veteran of World War II and had in fact been a POW (prisoner of war). Almost the entire crew of my aircraft was serving in the Air Force Reserve after fighting in WWII. To our great benefit, many of these veterans had now been deployed for active duty during the Korean War.

Aldhizer was approximately 30 years old and was actually a peanut farmer, extremely handsome, and six feet tall — what I perceived as the perfect stature for an Air Force pilot. By the professionalism, integrity, wisdom, strength and kindness he showed not just to his crew but anyone he met, Captain Aldhizer definitely became a hero to me and someone I would model myself after for years to come.

The captain informed us we were nearly ready to leave and that our relocation plan was to fly to Guam, but first we would stop in Honolulu, Hawaii.

We shipped out from Travis and headed for Honolulu, then took off for Andersen Air Force Base in Guam. However, it was not smooth sailing as we had expected.

After leaving Honolulu we lost the #4 engine on our B29 — the engine had swallowed an engine valve and stopped operating. When a valve breaks, small pieces can be ingested into the combustion chamber which destroys the top of the piston and cylinder head. You couldn't just replace the valve; a whole new engine had to be shipped to us from Honolulu.

That is how we ended up landing on Kwajalein Atoll in the Marshall Islands. Captain Aldhizer made the decision to stop there to wait for an engine to arrive. Little did we know then that we would have to wait three weeks for the replacement engine to arrive.

It was a wonderful time of rest. We were living in a screened-in cabin right on the water, and only a few steps away we could go for a swim. Every day we would eat wonderful food in a magnificent naval chow hall – the dining facility was a big highlight of this location -- and a different movie played almost every night outside under the stars. My buddies and I would get a drink -- usually bourbon and soda -- in the noncommissioned officers' quarters, go to dinner, then get another drink and some popcorn to take to the movies. It was quite a novel and fun experience.

While on the island, we were informed that a few hundred miles away the world's first thermonuclear weapon – the first H-bomb (hydrogen bomb) test was to be set off on Eniwetok Atoll in the Marshall Islands. Code named Mike, this was to occur on the Saturday of that first week – November 1, 1952. It was to go off at approximately 4:00 in the morning, and we were issued special glasses so we could sit in a trench and watch the set-off. When the bomb went off the entire island shook. It was a huge explosion, rising thousands of feet into the air and spreading out into a mushroom-shaped multicolored plume. It seemed to hang there for hours and then finally moved farther west out to the sea.

***

At last the engine arrived and was installed, and off we flew from our paradise post on Kwajalein Atoll to Tarague Beach on Andersen Air Force Base in Guam. B-29s were in action on all but 26 days during the war, some 35 months of combat, with a relatively small force of just over 100 bombers. There were twelve B-29 aircraft where we were stationed.

Inflight to Guam I noticed the new engine that had just been replaced was operating kind of rough, and it scared me a little bit, and it scared the captain too, actually.

When we landed we got off the airplane and Captain Aldhizer walked over to the propeller and reached up to grab it, and it came right off. If it had spun off while we were in the air, it could have caused untold damage.

That happened solely because the crew chief who had replaced the engine had failed to install one little part of it properly, the oil slinger ring. That's a thin metal disc that repels oil away from the crankshaft seal at high pressure and at a very high volume. He had made a terribly risky mistake, and the captain was livid. Once again, we lucked out.

Our job was to fly to Okinawa, load an A-bomb, and in rotation fly from there to the perimeter of South Korea and North Korea. In a twelve-hour period we would continuously fly around the island, then be relieved by another crew, their B-29 also loaded with an A-bomb. B-29s flew these 'round the clock missions accompanied by escort fighter aircraft, the F-80 Shooting Star and F-86 Sabre, which were designed to accompany bombers to and from targets.

Captain Aldhizer and the copilot, whenever they flew, wherever we went, there was always a bottle of Jack Daniels sitting between them. I'm not kidding, and it continually worried me - they would always take a swig from it on the way to the site that we were going to turn around on, and then again on the way back. And I thought, *'Well how can they fly, and fly perfectly?'* So I asked him one time, "How come you're drinking?" and he told me, "It helps calm our nerves." And I said, "Well, when did you start that?" and he replied, "I started that in the Pacific Islands in World War II. We drank every day."

The purpose of this exercise was that if President Truman ordered the dropping of an A bomb on the Chinese and North Koreans, we would be prepared to do so. Thank the good Lord the orders never came.

Living on Guam was an experience — hot, steamy, and very jungle-like. The food was horrible as everything was powdered, even the milk. Each aircraft was parked in the jungle on their own pad. Whenever you went to check on the aircraft, you might run into an eight-foot lizard, most likely a monitor lizard. It didn't seem to have teeth and ate just vegetation, and was not dangerous but they always scared the heck out of us. There were also tiny deer about two feet tall, possibly the Philippine deer.

We spent a lot of time in the service club at night. There was a very popular twenty-piece band called Pacifico Joe; they had learned how to play like Harry James, and a woman in the group sang exactly like Patty Page. They would make the circuit to Guam and other Pacific Islands. I'll never forget Pacifico Joe – they were really great entertainment.

I made a lot of friends there, as we were all pretty much stuck in the same place, and I especially remember my buddy Gary Nelson, who was also an Air Force flight engineer in our squadron but on a different plane. You can be sure all of us spent a lot of time in the service club at night, enjoying the music and atmosphere Pacifico Joe created for our pleasure. It's one of my fondest memories of serving in the Air Force in Guam.

Eventually, Truman decided he would bring MacArthur home. He was determined not to drop another A-bomb.

After approximately eight months on the island we were ordered to fly all 12 aircraft back to Travis Air Force Base. They were going to replace the B-29s with a new bomber called the B-47; it was a twin-engine jet bomber. The B-29s were to be retired to the junkyard, although I understand 22 B-29 airplanes are currently on display in various aviation museums, including the Castle Air Museum in Atwater, California. Of these 22, I believe only two are flyable.

A third divine intervention took place while we were flying home to Travis Air Force Base from Honolulu. I was sitting at my station in the Superfortress behind the copilot and pilot when I began smelling an acrid, almost acid-like smell and smoke in the cockpit. I noticed that the number-four engine had lost manifold power and dropped in oil pressure, and immediately notified the captain via the intercom.

He exclaimed, "We've got to cut that engine off. There's something terribly wrong."

I cut the prop and turned the engine off, but the smoke continued. In an emergency, there are procedures to follow in aviation terminology and practical risk management. In the cockpit there is an alarm system, warning bells the pilot can turn on that will be heard over the entire aircraft. If you discover that you are in trouble and need to recommend the crew put on their parachute backpacks, you ring alarm bell number one, an audible signal to draw the attention of all personnel onboard.

One of the airplane commander's first responsibilities before ever taking off is to train their crew for an emergency, including bailing out. Crew members must also know their duties, which hatch/exit to use, how to bail out and deploy their parachute to land on soil or sea, etc.

As the alarm bells were rung at first alarm, all crewmembers were encouraged to don our backpacks as we were informed we may have to abandon our Superfortress in flight. As the engineer, my duty was to assist the captain as directed. The navigator informed the radio operator of our exact location, and was prepared to send the distress call before each of us jumped.

We got into our backpack parachutes which had been stored in the back of the plane. Captain Aldhizer then rang alarm bell number two, which meant that now the pilot was going to point the nose of the aircraft down to drop from 25,000 feet to 10,000 feet, open the two bomb bay doors, and dump everything out to lighten the load in the plane. The captain felt that there possibly was a fire between the electrical connections in the wing and engine number four, and if that were the case, it could cause an explosion in the gas tank.

At that point we were somewhat panicked and started dumping everything we could out of the bomb bay. The B-29s had two weapons bays that held bombs, which would be opened when the bombs were ready to be dropped. Now though, we opened the bomb bay door to drop our extra weight.

The officers on the crew had purchased a large number of cases of Four Roses Whiskey at a good price and were taking them home. We dumped them. We also dumped over thirty or forty flight flak shields, which are used to line the interior of an aircraft to protect against getting shot up inside by either other aircraft or ground artillery.

A brigadier general was hitching a ride with us from Yokota, Japan and was seated in the rear of the aircraft, towards the tail. He was on his way home on leave and had purchased a beautiful chinchilla fur coat for his wife. I believe later he said it had cost him about $10,000. That coat was also in the bomb bay, but when we noticed the box we couldn't bring ourselves to toss it out, so we stuffed it inside the bomb bay compartment.

We were all of course wearing our oxygen masks, backpacks and headsets — it was the only way we could communicate with each other. The navigator noticed I had put on my parachute and asked me if I'd ever practiced jumping. I told him no, we had never gone through that particular practice in training. He kindly pointed out that I was wearing it backwards and helped me to correct that. He explained, not quite in these words, "If you jump wearing your chute like that, let's just say you won't be having any children in your future..."

He then proceeded to instruct me about jumping, describing the various survival gear I'd have available once I landed in the sea, including food, water, and shark repellant. The first and most important thing, he emphasized, was to disconnect my chute just before my feet hit the water by depressing the quick release box, as he demonstrated this to me. Otherwise the current would pull the parachute, and me, away.

Well, as you can imagine, as soon as I realized we may be jumping in with sharks, my decision was made: I would go down with the plane. I was completely terrified of all the possible ramifications of jumping ship.

The captain was getting ready to ring alarm bell three, which meant bail out. At that point the cockpit was totally full of smoke and we couldn't see each other it was so thick. I hate to relive that moment, it was so frightening.

Through our headsets we heard, "Is Benny the crew chief on board?" "Yes, he's in the back," I answered. The crewmen were housed aboard the aircraft in three segments: nose, waist and tail turret sections, connected by a communications tube. Crewmen could crawl through the joined nose and waist compartments cylinder that sat over the bomb bay to get back and forth as needed. Fortunately the three sections of our plane were pressurized separately and each one sealed off by doors, so the smoke hadn't traveled from the cockpit.

The captain asked me to crawl through the tube and bring Benny forward, which I did. I sat back at my station, and Benny came up to look at the instruments. He noticed that the pressure in engine number one was down. He also noticed that I had cut off the power to engine number four.

As he was talking to me, he placed one hand on a metal carriage located behind the pilot. Inside that carriage with a metal door were four turbo amplifiers. He immediately burned his hand and said, "Holy smokes, the amplifier's on fire!" He pulled a pair of gloves out of his pocket, grabbed the door and pulled it open. He saw the amplifier, unscrewed it to remove it and threw it out of the bomb bay, which was already open because of the planned bail out.

He instructed me, "There are two amplifiers under your seat that are spares. Give me one."

I pulled it out and he plugged it into the empty space, then told me to crank up engine number four, which I did. It started, and off we went, continuing our trek from Hawaii to Travis Air Force Base.

I'm certain the experience of almost the entire crew having the familiarity of warplanes after flying in WWII was a significant reason the plane and crew were saved that day.

Somehow, the press got ahold of our inflight dilemma and when our planes landed at Travis there was a bevy of media and press waiting for us. The brigadier general immediately made contact with each B-29 crew and ordered them to disembark the aircraft without any cargo. The last thing he wanted was for the press to see the collection of personal items we'd purchased for our loved ones, including the whiskey and his prized chinchilla. We did read about it afterwards in the San Francisco Chronicle.

A couple months later I received a call from the brigadier general that we were to receive an air medal award for saving the lives of our crew and the $30,000,000 aircraft, and most likely his wife's full length chinchilla coat.

Ray in Military Uniform (1950)

Sergeant Raymond C Simon, United States Air
Force, 1950-1954, Korean War Air Force career air
medals, including good conduct, national defense,
Korea, strategic air command, dog tag, stripes

Ray and his buddy, Air Force Flight Engineer Gary Nelson,
Tarague Beach on Andersen Air Force Base, Guam (1951)

The B29 Superfortress that Ray flew in as an engineer during
the Korean War (1952)

5

JOAN

My time in the Air Force was coming to a close. It was December 15, and I was to be honorably discharged on January 5, 1954. The major of our wing called and declared, "Sergeant Simon, we want you to stay in the Air Force, and we are willing to make you a great offer: a $10,000 bonus and an agreement in writing for you to go to any base in the world you choose." I told him the offer was generous, but no-soap – there was no chance of that happening; I was leaving. I got myself ready to go by packing everything up and began to load my car.

My parents had moved to Modesto during my time in the Air Force to be near my sister Mary and her husband Zen Damir, who lived here. When I was discharged, I realized I had no place to call home. I asked my parents if I could move in with them for a couple of years while I sorted out my future, and that's how I ended up in Modesto.

A lot of military personnel spent their youthful years they would normally be in college, serving our country. It was common for a freshman class to have a mixture of 18-year-olds amongst returning veterans 24 years of age or so. The impact was often very positive for both age groups: the veterans had a more mature, world view and tended to appreciate and realize the importance of obtaining an education, while the younger set were gifted with a more serious group of classmates whom they could emulate.

Finally "back home," I decided to enroll at Modesto Junior College, but I had to have a job until February 1st. I was discharged from the service with no money and needed something to live on, and I needed to qualify for the GI Bill to go to school.

In 1944 Franklin D. Roosevelt had signed into law the GI Bill of Rights, or Servicemen's Readjustment Act, after World War II to provide benefits to veterans returning to college with tuition, low interest small business loans, housing, and unemployment benefits. GI stands for general issue or government issue, and soldiers started referring to themselves as GIs.

The first thing I needed was a job, so I went to the Employment Development Department to see what might be available and found a job opportunity at the Continental Can Company, which was the world's largest packaging company. I worked the graveyard shift lifting 25-pound rolls of tin into a can making machine. The cans were shipped everywhere, and our local canneries made great use of them as you can imagine.

This job, as disagreeable as it was for me at the time,

definitely added to making me the person I am today. I learned to respect that not everyone has the chance or choice to gain an education, learn a craft, or find the job that inherently fits them. While I already had a great appreciation for the fortunate life I had led to this point, this job humbled me with even more appreciation for my fellow man. I stayed with Continental Can until school started.

Later on when summer was approaching, my brother-in-law Zen helped me get a job with the California Cling Peach Advisory Board as a grader at the Hughson Station, which was a centralized grading station with all the major fruit canners renting space. Zen and his father owned and operated their farming business, growing peaches as a main crop.

The farmers would deliver their fruit to the various grading stations and we'd look at each variety of peach for quality of color (they couldn't be too green or too ripe), size, and visible damage from insects. To size the peaches we'd choose samples from each load to manually fit over a 2-3/8" brass ring, one at a time.

If the peach passed through the ring, the fruit was too small and in that case we would have to reject the load. The farmer then had to take the peaches back to their orchard and re-sort them, then return them to us appropriately sorted for another grade. At times, the farmer would elect to dump a particular load instead of going through the process again.

It was a great opportunity and I had a job during the summer every year thereafter. If you worked overtime, which I generally did, you could make a few thousand dollars per summer. That, added to my G.I. Bill easily put me through four years of college.

Back then, while grading peaches, I worked with Milton David. He was studying medicine and constantly reading medical books. Eventually he became Dr. Milton David, an orthopedic surgeon here in Modesto.

One particular season I met a very interesting gentleman who was one of the larger peach growers. He would occasionally drive his own peach jitney into the grading station, and I remember noticing he always had the most peaches. He was a well-known and successful Modesto businessman; Hashem Naraghi.

Hashem was the personification of an entrepreneur. Besides being a captivating conversationalist, he was extremely gregarious. One day I noticed he was wearing one of the most beautiful rings I'd ever seen. In the center was a huge diamond and it was embellished with engravings on each side. He told me it was given to him by Mohammad Reza Shah Pahlavi, the last Shah of Iran, who was partners with Hashem in his agricultural business in Iran; at one time they had owned quite a lot of farmland together.

Hashem was married to a beautiful Persian woman, Nora, and they had three delightful and intelligent children: a son, Wendell, who became an attorney and was in business with his father — I remember when he married a girl named Peggy — and beautiful and accomplished daughters, Margaret and Sharon.

After working with him for a while and getting to

know him, he relayed to me his story of leaving Iran. The Shah had warned him one day, "You should leave Iran. They are after me and if they find me will probably depose or kill me. You need to leave because you have shared too much information, and they will most likely hang you as well."

Hashem had come to Modesto to be free from the threat of the Shah's opposition, and for the opportunity living in the United States would bring him and his family. Using money from selling his land in Iran, Hashem was interested in land development and continually searched for land to buy all around the Modesto area, and also continued his farming, planting peach orchards.

I enjoyed getting to know the Naraghis and we became good friends. My son Jeff and I were often invited to their beautiful home to hunt pheasants on the surrounding acreage, although Hashem didn't enjoy hunting. He had done very well for himself, and had built a magnificent mansion with a man-made lake east of Turlock. As I recall, he also owned quite a large amount of property, a huge apartment on Nob Hill, a home on the lake at Lake Tahoe, and another on the river at Masonic Park in Santa Cruz. He'd often invite us to stay at his apartment in San Francisco, which was glorious.

Joan and I were invited to functions at his home where we met the Shah's sister, the Princess Fatemeh Pahlavi, with her husband, a four-star general from Iran.

We learned that Fatemeh had first been married for about 10 years to a local gentleman, Vincent Hillyer of Los Banos, while he was a student at Harvard Medical School.

But because she did not get the Shah's permission first, her royal privileges were taken from her.

Subsequently, however, she married the commander of Iran's Air Force, and at this time they were hiding out in Modesto from the extremist groups. Years later, the general returned to Iran and was "suspiciously killed" in a flying accident. The Shah died from cancer in 1980 while in exile in Cairo, Egypt.

We had also met a gentleman named John Amos at an event at the Naraghi home and became friends. John was a very wealthy businessman and well known – he and his brothers had founded American Family Life Insurance Company in the 1950s. Eventually the company became American Family Life Assurance Company of Columbus – Aflac.

On one trip to Washington, D.C., Joan and I were in the Nation's Capital having lunch with California Congressman John McFall (1956-1978), who was from Manteca, California. He represented the northern Central Valley, and eventually became House Majority Whip.

During our meal I exclaimed to Joan, "Isn't that John Amos sitting across the room?" Sure enough, it was. I got up and walked over and said, "Hello John." Was I surprised when he replied, "Ray Simon, Stanislaus County Board of Supervisors." I couldn't believe he'd have all of that at the tip of his tongue.

When I got back to our table John McFall asked me, "You know John Amos? Can you introduce me to him?" and I did. I had a good laugh about that. Representative McFall was well liked and knew everyone, yet he needed me to make an introduction to one of the most powerful men of that time.

———————

While working my peach grading job I entered Modesto Junior College under the liberal arts program, as I was intending to transfer to the University of California, Berkeley once I got my associates degree. I worked very hard at school; I was taking eighteen units, and because I had been away from school so long, I was fearful I might not be successful. As it turned out, I was a straight A student that first quarter, and virtually continued that trend into the next year. I did also take a class for extra units in dramatic arts because it was a very natural thing for me and I thought it would be easy to pick up, and fun.

Over those two years I was in several plays, the main one being a musical by American author and playwright Booth Tarkington called *Seventeen*. A well-known author and playwright, Tarkington claims the prestige of being one of only four novelists to win the Pulitzer Prize for Fiction multiple times.

This is where I met Joan. I had been attracted to her all the time I went to my dramatics class in that she was extremely beautiful, and diminutive. I was not the only one who liked her. Buck Townsend, who went on to become an opera singer in New York and sang professionally in North America and Europe as Lead Tenor before returning to Modesto to found and direct the Townsend Opera Players, kept saying to me, "Every one of us resents the fly-boy coming home to steal our girl!"

Joan likes to tell the story of how we finally started dating. We didn't get to know each other right away; she seemed like a nice person and was very pretty, but I was rather shy and didn't have the courage to talk with her.

It wasn't until our drama instructor, Mr. Frank DeLamater, took our class on a field trip to San Francisco to see Burgess Meridith's *The Teahouse of The August Moon* at the Curran Theatre.

Joan rode on the bus with her friends Caroline Coleman and Marilyn Dutra, and they sat together all throughout the show. Afterwards the bus dropped the class off at the Cliff House Restaurant for dinner.

I didn't know anyone and I saw Joan sitting with her friends, so I asked, "Could I sit with you ladies?"

"Sure," they responded.

Well, we talked through dinner and it was an easy conversation, like we'd known each other for ages. When we got back on the bus for the drive home, the other girls sat together and Joan sat in a seat by herself. I asked, "May I sit with you?" and she acquiesced. We talked all the way home while everyone else fell asleep.

Joan told her mother about it when she got home and she exclaimed, "Joan, he likes you." Joan didn't know about that, but it had been a very nice day. She admitted later that she secretly hoped I would ask her out.

But I didn't right away. It was a few months before I eventually got up the nerve to ask her out, but she told me no; she already had a date for that night. Well I thought she just wasn't interested in me, so that was it – I was not going to humiliate myself asking her again just to be told no.

Several months went by before we were cast together in this play, Booth Tarkington's *Seventeen*, both of us as the leads. At every rehearsal we'd sit across from each other doing our makeup, talking. During rehearsal Mr. DeLamater would scold us that our scene was not right, and send us to the practice room to rehearse it. Well, we talked more than we rehearsed.

Joan was working at JCPenney's part time, and her mother would pick her up from work to drop her off at rehearsal. We normally finished around 9:30 at night and Joan would always call her mother to pick her up. One night she mentioned she hadn't called yet for a ride home, and I told her I'd take her, so I did.

The next day when her mother dropped her off, she asked Joan, "Do you want me to pick you up tonight?" Joan could hear her mother chuckling when she asked that question, knowing what the answer would be. Of course, Joan told her, "I'll call you when I'm done." As you might have already figured out, Joan would casually mention to me that she had to call her mother and I'd always offer to drive her home. She confessed later that I was so timid, she had to make it happen. Now Joan tells everyone, "And he's been taking me home ever since."

After we had gone together for approximately a year and a half, I asked her if she would marry me while sitting in my car in front of her house. She was excited about my proposal and wanted to tell her parents right away.

Upon graduation from junior college, however, we were going to be separated. I was going to the University of California at Berkeley — the School of Criminology to be exact — and it would be a two-year stint. In my mind, I needed to graduate with a degree before getting married.

Joan, meanwhile, had a scholarship to the University of the Pacific and planned to pursue a degree in education. I used to stop in Stockton to pick her up on my drive home from Cal, and drop her off at her parents' home on weekends. I would stay at my mother's house.

W orking towards my degree at UC Berkeley's School of Criminology, I had some of the most interesting and famous instructors in the world. Charles O'Neill, inventor of the O'Neill system of fingerprinting which was used all over the world, taught the class on fingerprinting.

My class in criminal psychiatry was taught by Lt. Colonel Douglas M Kelley, MD, a US Army Military Intelligence Corps Officer who was the chief psychiatrist at the Nuremberg Trials. His patients included Nazi General Hermann Goering, head of the German Air Force, and also the Deputy Fuhrer to Adolf Hitler, Rudolph Hess.

The purpose of the Nuremberg Trials which were held from 1945-1949 were to bring Nazi war criminals to justice.

The defendants included Nazi Party officials, high ranking military officers, and German lawyers, doctors, and industrialists who had been indicted on charges of crimes against peace and humanity. These trials are considered significant regarding establishing a permanent international court.

Kelley wrote two books about the Nuremberg trials: The Case of Rudolph Hess (Kelley came to the conclusion that Hess suffered "a true psychoneurosis, primarily of the hysterical type, engrafted on a basic paranoid and schizoid personality, with amnesia, partly genuine and partly feigned."), and Twenty-two Cells in Nuremberg.

Dr. Kelley would tell us many stories about the Nazi prisoners' treatment, as the authorities apparently wanted to make sure that all of these criminals understood that they were being tried and would be executed for the atrocities they had committed.

The prisoners were searched every day for anything that might allow them to commit suicide. One main method was using something called potassium cyanide, and if you took just one pill you would expire within seconds. The United States also issued this pill to CIA agents who had overseas assignments; they could easily swallow one to avoid being tortured for information in case they got caught.

One particularly interesting story Kelley told us was of guards rushing into his office one day saying that Goering had killed himself. Dr. Kelley immediately went to the cell and found that Goering had taken the potassium cyanide compound. The date was October 15, 1946. Goering had concealed two tablets in a metal capsule within his body. In fact, he had only taken one, so there was one pill left in the case. Dr. Kelly admitted he admired that Goering had control over his own death, something that left quite an impression on him.

In class one day, Dr. Kelley held up the actual small container that had been found on Hermann Goering and he showed us the little pink pill of potassium cyanide. Sadly, it was that same pill that Dr. Kelley took during my last year in school. He used it to take his own life in front of his wife, father and oldest son while he was fixing dinner at his home New Year's Day 1958. When I read about it in the newspaper, it was the most devastating incident of my life. I had a great deal of respect for this man and was thunderstruck as to how he could do such a thing.

After all these years, I began thinking about him and realized that he alone was a person who, as a criminal psychiatrist widely known and world-famous, had testified against murderers and other criminals in cases where he found his patients to be psychopaths suffering from violent social behavior; aggressive and unstable, possibly incapable of understanding that what they had done was completely depraved.

I fully believe that all of these testimonies weighed so heavily on him that it just became too much to cope with. At some point, Kelley became an alcoholic and despondent.

We had many other famous instructors from around the United States in criminal law. Some were federal justices, and others were defense attorneys, such as Melvin Belli from San Francisco.

During our spare time in the afternoon and evening, several of my friends and I decided to enter the Alameda County Sheriff's Office academy to study basic police officer training. We each put in over four hundred hours and became Sheriff's deputies. Sheriff H.P. (Jack) Gleason gave us our badges at the promotional ceremony, and that day remains a highlight of my life in the period when I was a young college student working to achieve my dream.

I should mention at this point that while I was in my last year at college, I went home one weekend to pick Joan up and take her back to her house in Modesto. When we went out that evening, she said to me, "Ray, I want to get married now. We have been apart far too long, and I can't stand this too much longer." I agreed it was time for us to get married, and we set the date at August 31, 1957. We immediately began to look for an apartment in Berkeley so we could live there after the wedding.

We got married in the Lutheran Church in Modesto. Our pastor, Carl Erickson, it turns out, had navigated supply planes during WWII and also the Korean Conflict.

He was a Swedish man who had a hard time with English, and as we were a bit giddy from all the excitement of the day, we found that quite amusing. At the end of the ceremony, as he blessed us, he spoke, "In the name of the Father, and of the Son, and of the Holy 'Sport' — which had us smiling, trying not to laugh as he was a very respectable man and we didn't want to embarrass him.

My best man was Paul Hansen and Joan's maid of honor was Mary Van Konynenburg, both friends of ours from high school. The rest of our wedding party included Joan's bridesmaids Marianne Corson (Giddings) and Karen Nelson, my groomsmen Jerry Sather, a friend from junior college, along with Gary Brown, Lee Mealey, and Leo McDermott. Joan's younger brother, Steve Pedego, and her cousins Duane and Ronald Nelson acted as acolytes and were our candle lighters. They would have been teenagers at the time, probably in high school.

Joan's parents hosted our wedding reception in their backyard for about 300 guests. My good friend George Giddings had married Joan's good friend Marianne Corson, the Modesto Junior College President's daughter. George was a terrific guy, however, he didn't leave a great impression with the ladies of the church. Joan's mother had helped them make a wonderful punch, and the ladies were quite irritated when they found that George had spiked it with vodka.

When we finally left for our honeymoon in Lake Tahoe, my best man Paul Hansen handed us a bottle of Champagne on our way out the door at about 10:00 p.m. with congratulations and orders to enjoy ourselves.

For our honeymoon, my dad offered us his Buick Super which was probably a 1954 or '55. Buick's focus with the

Supers was comfort and we were thrilled to be granted the use of this fine automobile.

It had been an eventful day and we got as far as Lodi when I told Joan I just couldn't drive any further, as we had about a three- or four-hour drive ahead of us. We stopped at a motel in Lodi and got a room. I told Joan, "Let's open the Champagne." Unfortunately the bottle was warm, so we placed it in the toilet tank's cool water to chill a little bit. We ended up drinking the whole bottle, and in the morning headed to our destination, Lake Tahoe.

Driving past Sacramento we noticed the California State Fair was in progress, and decided it might be fun to make another stop on our way. As luck would have it, we happened to see someone who had been at the wedding. When she saw us she stated, "My gosh you guys look terrible the day after your wedding."

"What do you mean?" we asked her.

"You both have dark circles under your eyes. You must have had some wedding night."

We still have a good laugh about that when we think of it.

We stayed in Tahoe for three or four days and I remember our hotel was $12.00 per night. We saw a stage show with Tony Martin, a popular actor and singer since the 1930s, but when we went to look at the slot machines at Harrah's Casino we got kicked out because Joan looked too young.

We found a very nice apartment in Berkeley not too far from the school. Joan got a job in Oakland with the telephone company, and I worked after school three days a week for Hink's Department Store on Shattuck Avenue as a floor walker, with the customary carnation in my lapel which I found amusing. Large department stores used to employ floor walkers, whose job was to walk around directing customers to their desired destination in the store, supervising sales, and generally being a welcoming and helpful force.

When I lived in Berkeley before Joan and I got married, I had a roommate. His name was Leo McDermott. It turned out that Leo had an uncle named Leo Carrillo who came to visit him in Berkeley occasionally, and this Leo Carrillo was a well-known movie star whose character was The Cisco Kid's partner, Pancho. Every once in a while, he would come to Berkeley and take us out to dinner and tell us all about the scandals in Hollywood.

Believe it or not, the maid of honor from our wedding, Mary, and my best man, Paul, started corresponding with each other after the wedding, and ultimately we attended their wedding before they moved to Edmonds, Washington. Paul became a superior court judge and Mary, a mother of four children. Unfortunately, Paul just passed away at age eighty-eight, while I'm dictating this story.

Joan and I found as we grew to know each other that we shared some common and also very strange coincidences. Of course our love of performing in the theatre arts is what put Joan and me together, and it was interesting to learn that both of us at the age of five were performing in public. My parents had entered me in a singing contest in Conrad, which I won, and Joan was dancing the hula at a dance contest at her hometown Strand Theatre, which she won as well. Built in 1920, The Strand is now the site of Brenden Theatres in downtown Modesto.

One thing that was unsettling at first was when we were comparing notes of relatives. Someone at our wedding had given us a heritage book and once we started filling it out, we learned that Joan's paternal grandmother was named Myrtle Wheeler. Well, my maternal grandmother was also named Myrtle Wheeler. Myrtle was a pretty popular name in the late 1800s into the early 1900s. Thankfully they were not related, but you can believe it gave us pause.

Another interesting coincidence is that we were both raised in the Lutheran Church, and both were born in a St. Mary's Hospital, albeit mine was in Conrad, and hers Modesto. By chance, our granddaughter Jessica was born in the same hospital as Joan, 53 years later.

St. Mary's Hospital became a very welcoming place for me growing up. Whenever I'd want to get a drink of water or a soda, or just a hug and a friendly face, I'd go see the Catholic Nun Sister Liola. I'll never forgot her kindness to me, her genuine love, her generosity, and her friendship. She was like a grandmother to me, and we remained friends for many years.

In Conrad, Pastor Stime baptized me into the Lutheran Church and when I was a little older I was also assistant to the Pastor reading scripture every Sunday, which was a big deal for me as a youngster. Most likely my parents saw that as an excellent way of teaching me scripture without me realizing it.

In our Modesto Lutheran Church, Pastor Segerhammer

approached me one day after services and asked if I would be interested in being a Sunday school teacher to the 7th or 8th graders, so for that one year I taught. Years later, a young lady walked up to me and asked if I remembered her. She did look familiar, and I found that she was the Stanislaus County Deputy District Attorney and was one of the students I had taught in the 60s.

Her name is Carol Shipley and although she's retired recently from being assistant district attorney, she was one of our county's finest and most conscientious public servants in the years that she served, and it was a pleasure getting to know her as an adult and working with her. She also had been assigned to Crimes Against Children, something I've been passionate about fighting most of my adult life.

MJC Musical *Seventeen* cast — Ray and Joan first met as the
male and female leads (1955)

MJC Musical *Seventeen* — Center: Joan is holding
the dog's leash, and Ray is standing in a tuxedo just
past Joan's left shoulder (1955)

Ray and Joan on their wedding day

Ray and Joan on their wedding day, leaving for their
honeymoon

6

THE CENTRAL INTELLIGENCE
AGENCY: CIA

Graduation was right around the corner. When the day came, it was held in the Berkeley football stadium. There were over a thousand graduates from various departments.

Near the last day of school, just before graduation, I was called into the dean's office by Dr. Alonzo W. Wilson who had been a chief spy for the Allied nations in Western Europe during World War II. He asked, "What do you plan on doing after graduation, Ray?"

I stated that at this time, I did not know.

He said, "The CIA is recruiting on campus, and I believe you would qualify for that position — the one they're looking to fill. If you're interested, I will give your phone number to this gentleman, and he will call you for an appointment."

I gave him my phone number, and the next day got a phone call. The man told me, "I will meet you on University Avenue in front of the Safeway store and will be driving a '50s tan Chevrolet."

I walked to the corner and he drove up in the Chevy, but then drove by me not once but twice. He finally came around again and stopped and motioned me over to the car. He explained that we were going to drive down by the bay to the CHP driving course where law enforcement learns defensive driving: skid pan training, high speed crash avoidance, and low speed precision maneuvering.

We drove down to that area, and he chatted with me for a while then handed me a number of papers and said, "You can go home after I drop you off. Complete these and mail them in."

I went home and filled the papers out. They asked for a lot of personal information about my family and Joan's. I mailed the papers in and waited. Finally, I got a letter back that was devastating to me. It simply said, "We regret to inform you that because your mother-in-law is foreign-born, we could not accept your application."

Joan's mother was born in Sweden and had come to America with her mother when she was 12 years old. This particular line seemed ridiculous to me, but of course I then began searching for another job. Three or four days had passed when I received a telephone call from the man in the Chevy. He said, "We would like to talk with you. Could you come to San Francisco? Go to the Flood Building which is right across from Nordstrom on Market Street; second floor, room 200."

He gave me a day to make my decision, and when I did, I drove to San Francisco and went to the Flood

Building to the second floor as he had instructed. When I opened the door, I saw nothing. The office was an empty space but I could hear some murmuring coming from the room next door. I opened the door to that room, and there were three gentlemen sitting around a table.

The fellow I had met in the Chevrolet said, "Come in, Mr. Simon. We would like to talk with you and explain." He told me that the rules were firm, but they had run it by a number of officials in Langley, Virginia, and made a determination that I was still the best candidate. This man's job was interviewing and vetting prospective employees for Seattle City Schools. The job would be unique as I would officially be on the City Schools' payroll and working under the Security Chief, who was going to be in Seattle. He said they had specific criteria for hiring: they wanted someone who had a degree in criminology, the discipline of the military service, looked young enough to pass as a high school senior, and had some police training. You can be sure that now I was very glad to have put in the effort while in college to take those 400 hours of Deputy Sheriff classes at the Alameda County Sheriff's Training Center.

However, I had been under the impression that if you were going into the CIA, you could not be employed or serve within the continental limits, that it would be a foreign assignment, and I mentioned this to him.

He said, "No, that is all changed, for this reason." He explained that the President of the United States, Dwight D. Eisenhower (1953-1961), had issued a Presidential

Directive that immediately started the CIA operating domestically.

A Presidential Directive is an executive order, not legislation, and therefore does not require approval from Congress; thus it cannot be overturned by Congress.

Eisenhower had made a decision to bring all of his old friends from the OSS (the Office of Strategic Services) which was the intelligence agency during World War II, into its replacement: the new CIA (Central Intelligence Agency), which had been formed in 1952.

The CIA, in turn, established over four hundred storefronts — operating offices — in each of the states, and Operation Chaos, a domestic espionage project which pursued possible foreign influence, was born. The purpose of choosing Seattle was that Washington was the only state in the Union that forbade the establishment of communist cells.

At the Department of Justice, J. Edgar Hoover was an enthusiastic young employee and quickly ascended the ranks of the DOJ. After his first year he was promoted to assistant to the attorney general, in the next year he led the Department's General Intelligence Division. Two years later he was named the assistant director of the Bureau of Investigation, and within three years reached the designation of the first director of the FBI, which he held from age 29 until his death at age 77.

He was known for strengthening the FBI, modernizing police technology (fingerprint files; forensic laboratories – the largest in the world), and establishing a black list (now called the Terrorist Screening Database).

However, J. Edgar Hoover was also notoriously known as being very controversial in his tactics to collect detrimental information on politicians and did not hesitate to use that data to threaten and intimidate officials, including sitting presidents.

In fact, even President Eisenhower learned that J. Edgar Hoover had been keeping a secret dossier on him, from the time Eisenhower was supreme commander of the Allied forces.

I was to go to Seattle to meet with Dr. Brock, superintendent of the Seattle Public Schools District. I would receive further instruction from my handler in Seattle, station chief Charles Barton, who was actually working in the crab shack on the campus of the University of Washington. The CIA had recruited people from all walks of life in the United States to serve domestically, including students, doctors, lawyers, and all kinds of working people.

When I went to see Barton, he informed me that I would be working undercover. Very few people would know: the school superintendent, as well as a couple of principals and teachers of high schools as needed, and Dewey Gillespie, chief detective for the Seattle Police Department. Also included was Francis Walter, the chair of the House Un-American Activities Committee in Washington, D.C. (1955-1963).

The House Committee on Un-American Activities (HCUA) was an investigative committee of the United States House of Representatives. From its inception in 1938 to becoming a permanent committee in 1945, it then came to be known as the House Committee on Internal Security in 1969. When the House abolished the committee in 1975, its role was transferred to the House Judiciary Committee. The purpose of the committee was to investigate alleged disloyalty and subversive activities of anyone suspected of having communist ties.

I accepted the position and was informed that I had no arrest powers as an operative. All arrests, if any, would be done by the Seattle PD. I was to tell Joan that I was working for the Seattle School District as an investigator. Besides my payroll coming through the school district, I would be supplied with a government-issued automobile with a two-way radio. I was cautioned that I could never discuss with Joan anything I did within my purview as an operative.

My first job at the end of 1958 and into 1959 was to enter Ballard High School as a senior transfer student and begin collecting evidence as to who was establishing student communist cell groups and find out where they were being held. I was of course working under cover and used an alias. I dressed as the other students – in cords (corduroy pants) that everyone would write all over with pens. I remember thinking to myself, 'Was I really this immature in high school?'

I enrolled in several classes and believed that the first people you wanted to get to know were the transfer students. They seemed to be the most desirable targets in school as they appeared to have not made many friends yet, being new, and might be easily influenced. But that wasn't true; those kids were alright. It was the kids who'd been there most of their lives, who were entrenched in the school and community, and knew which kids to target and manipulate.

I had to be as invisible as possible so I sat, very withdrawn, in the back of the classroom. The Principal at Ballard knew who I was, and the teacher knew; they both took care of keeping my cover to conceal who I really was and each day I only went to one class.

The only questions I received was from a group of girls who were suspicious of my unwillingness to fully integrate with the other kids. "We don't understand why you don't go to our dances, or date any of the girls," they complained. You can imagine what they thought when I declined their invitations.

I was finally invited to attend my first cell meeting in the home of one of the boys. They discussed the importance of Karl Marx and how democracies were corrupt. Each meeting was different with a variety of outside adult speakers. I recorded them all surreptitiously. I wore the recorder in my pockets, t-shirt, and taped to my torso, and had to buy new tapes each time I'd send a recorded tape into headquarters.

There were five cells and after I finished the first cell, I continued on to the second. There would be speakers, generally adults from the docks: Harry Bridges' longshoremen. Harry Bridges had emigrated to the U.S. from Australia, and is historically known as one of the most influential labor leaders in America. The boys discussed tactics in disruption. The next cell was research on upcoming event opportunities, and the last was organization on action. All of the recordings were sent to Langley.

I worked through three Seattle County schools at different times and was able to identify all five communist cell groups. Most of the students in that group were arrested and sent to the King County Juvenile Detention Center by the Seattle Police Department.

There were two students in particular that they were interested in. The boys attended Ballard High School and were apparently good friends. I learned that they had been distributing pornography throughout different schools and getting paid for it. It was a method of fundraising by the Communist Party for the communist cell groups. Unfortunately, a lot of it was child pornography.

I had been at work approximately five months when I found all of these pieces of information to be true. I got the address of one of the boys and passed it along to Dewey Gillespie. He told me that he wanted to go to the house but had to secure a search warrant first.

It was a Friday afternoon, and I knew I had to pick Joan up from her job at the telephone company where she was a line planner for AT&T. The time was about quarter to five, and I was supposed to meet Gillespie at five o'clock p.m. at the home. I hurried and picked Joan up and drove her into the alley behind the house we were going to search. I told her to lock the doors and never open them for anyone. She was reading a book at the time and never bothered to ask me what we were searching for.

We went into the house with a search warrant and found that the parents were not at home. We could find nothing after searching all the rooms.

I looked at Detective Gillespie and said, "If you were a young boy and you didn't want your parents to find you had these kinds of pictures, where would you hide them?"

We looked at each other and said, "Under the mattress."

In the boy's room, I lifted up the mattress and underneath were hundreds of pictures in glossy black and white. We knew we had it then.

It turned out that this boy was the leader. He told us where the other boy could be found and we had him picked up too.

Gillespie left a copy of the search warrant in the house with a note to the boy's parents saying that their son had been arrested and was being transferred to juvenile hall.

The next morning, I got a call from Dewey Gillespie who said he'd learned where the boys had gotten the pictures. He told me there was a four-story brick apartment house next door to their home, and the gentleman who lived there had a basement full of photos, including a studio set up with dressing rooms, cameras, lights, and about nineteen double-stack filing cabinets full of photo negatives. He said "We are going to make a raid on the apartment house tomorrow at four o'clock a.m."

I got to the apartment house a little before 4:00 the next morning, and there were probably fifteen officers waiting in front. They knocked on the door, and the gentleman in the house came to the door, after having gotten out of bed.

He asked, "What are you doing here? What do you want?"

Officer Gillespie responded, "We want to look in your basement."

The fellow asked, "What on earth for?"

Gillespie simply replied, "Come with me." And he opened the door.

The man we were talking to had a Russian surname and was the head of Seattle City Light, the public utility providing electricity to Seattle.

We all walked into the basement and were astounded at what we saw, as the description given to us by the boy was absolutely correct. A phone call was made to Public Works, and four giant trucks immediately arrived to load up the filing cabinets. It took almost all day to load and unload the files.

During the morning hours as they were loading, I did some exploring in the garage behind the building and found the fellow's car. I went back into the house and got his keys, as I had discovered a brand-new four-door Cadillac sedan parked inside. In the trunk of the car was a full complement of dried foods, several guns, and quite a few maps. In the glove compartment I found letters written to the man we had just arrested from various people across the United States, ordering certain kinds of film from him. Many of the people were employed by large corporations as field men, as best as I could ascertain.

We learned there was another house in Seattle in which these films were being processed and decided to make a raid on that house as well. It was a small house in the center of Seattle — I don't remember the exact street — and two gentlemen were in the home when we arrived. We showed them a search warrant and began searching the house but could find nothing.

I had an idea that maybe there was access to an attic and asked the owner of the house if he had a ladder, and he said he did. I found the ladder in the back hallway, brought it out into the front hallway, and climbed up through the ceiling opening to look in the attic. Lo and behold, there were hundreds of stacks of film up there. I leaned down through the opening to look into the hallway and yelled, "I found the other film."

Just as I did, I found myself looking into a double-barrel shotgun held by a man standing in the hallway below with his sights on me. I simply looked down the barrel of that gun and thought to myself, 'I'm going to die in a few seconds. My head is going to get blown off, and Joan will never know what happened to me.' At that instant a police officer rounded the corner, saw the man and grabbed him from behind by the arms; the shotgun went off into the floor. To me, that was my next example of divine intervention.

A ll of the people involved in the pornography ring were sent to prison after trials in front of Judge John Simmons in the Superior Court of Seattle. A few weeks later, Gillespie of the Seattle PD called me and said that the leader of the group was in the Whatcom

County Jail in Bellingham, Washington and wanted to talk to me briefly. I wasn't sure that I should, but I did tell Dewey, "If you go with me, I'll go."

He drove with me to Bellingham and we walked into an interview room. There sat this gentleman at the desk. He said to me, "So you're Ray Simon."

I said, "Yes."

He said, "You're a dead man, and so is your wife. We know where she lives, where she eats, where she has her hair done, how she travels, and everything about her. You both will be gone soon, because you have interrupted an international organization."

I was outed! I left there rather shaken, to be honest. I called Langley and said, "What am I going to do?" The assistant director told me they were going to take it up and would call me back.

They did call me back and said they were going to have to ship me out of the country. They said they would give me a commission as a lieutenant commander in the Navy and send me to the Embassy in Saigon. They would send Joan back to Modesto, and a female agent would be with her constantly for approximately twelve months. They would pay for everything in terms of her care and comfort. I could not tell her what was going on and could not tell her when I would be back.

I said, "Why Saigon?"

They said, "Because you speak French, and that's what they speak."

Historically, Napoleon had made the decision in 1857 to invade Vietnam, so French was spoken in Vietnam under

French colonial rule from late 1859 until 1954 when the Vietnamese Nationalist Ho Chi Minh led a four-month siege which resulted in the French leaving the region. From that point forward, the use of the French language declined to what is estimated to be only about 1% of the Vietnamese population that speak French today. This account also explains how Saigon was renamed Ho Chi Minh City.

I went home rather depressed and finally said to myself, 'I can't possibly do that to Joan — send her home to her parents while I'm shipped off to Saigon — never!'

I called Langley back and said, "I'm going to quit right now, and I'm going to move home."

He said, "That's your choice, and we thank you for your service. We suggest, however, that in our experience you need to stay as visible as possible when you go home. The reason is that these people do not like to do anything to people of high visibility. If you need help, call me."

That night, I told Joan that I had quit my job and was going to move back to Modesto if she would agree. She said, "Of course, but I'd just gotten used to Seattle and have made some friends. Why?"

I replied, "Joan, this job is going nowhere, and I'm never going to advance myself through life working this position." She finally agreed, and home we went.

CIA Special Agent badge, 1958-1960

Seattle Police Department Security Officer badge,
1958-1960

Award from the Central Intelligence Agency, CIA Agent 1958-
1960, Code "Cypher"

7

MODESTO

Well, we left Berkeley and relocated back to Modesto, to Joan's parents, Signe and Benny Pedego, as they had invited us to move in with them. We ended up living there for a brief period of time though, because soon enough I had the good fortune of receiving a phone call about a job.

Right away we moved into an apartment, and after working for a bit of time when I felt established in my new career, my dad and Joan's offered to help us to build a home of our own. With their assistance we were able to accomplish that. Joan's father did all the plaster work on this house, and the next one that we were to eventually build. This first house was on Hampshire Lane and was a three-bedroom ranch-style home, about 1,500 square feet. We had a living room and family room each with a fireplace, a dinette, and a pink kitchen. I helped put in the yard, and frankly, we had a very nice home that we ended up living in for about 12 years.

The call I'd gotten was from an insurance agent named Henry Laws about a firm called Freese & Gianelli that was looking for an investigator. Henry's wife was my sister's best friend; that's how he knew of me.

I went down for an interview with Louis "Bud" Gianelli and we hit it off, for one reason because he was a Cal graduate (University of California at Berkeley), as was I, and he also knew I'd had experience in investigations. Little did I know he would become like a brother to me.

Once I joined Ogden Freese and Bud Gianelli at Freese & Gianelli, which Ogden had founded in 1942, there were only the three of us. Ogden had taken Bud in as a partner, and then Bud hired me. As the story will tell, I stayed for over fifty years.

Bud was the finest person I've ever known my entire life, and we became the best of friends. I've never met anyone as intelligent, energetic, dedicated, and as much of a big brother as he was. He taught me a lot about business investigation and life in general. He was a full supporter, 100 percent, of myself and my family. I thoroughly enjoyed working for him, and I enjoyed my job. I put many hard hours into making sure that he knew I was for the company and the company's success.

In my training he wanted me to specialize in medical malpractice claims as they had a huge portfolio of companies that insured hospitals and doctors. One of the hospitals was our Stanislaus County Hospital. If we had an incident reported to insurance, Bud and Ogden handed that to me and I investigated it.

In order for me to become proficient in medical liabilities I went to the hospital library every day and read as many medical books as I could, so if I had to take a statement for a hospital or employee, I would know how to interpret what they were saying. There was a particular publication that I always read – Massachusetts General Hospital's newsletter. Research at Mass General began over 200 years ago and they had a hospital-based research program. I got most of my information, the best, most up-to-date information, from that newsletter.

I became proficient in medical terminology and was personally requested by a number of hospitals' insurers, and thus became acquainted with many doctors whose claims I was handling. I met quite a lot of people adjusting claims in property and liability, and really loved what I was doing.

If you knew Bud, there's no question why he was so admired and loved. He was an exceptional mentor and set a great example for many people. Here is just a fraction of why so many found him incomparable:

Early on in his career as an independent adjuster Bud represented insurance companies, but his heart was really with the people in Stanislaus, San Joaquin, and Tuolumne County. He spent a lot of time on the road visiting people who had lost their home or were injured in an accident, adjusting claims. He had that way about him; he cared about his customers and made a great effort to go to them to make what might have been a catastrophic time, as easy as possible. He always went above and beyond for the people, and he received a lot of respect and accolades for that.

When Bud was in his 40s, he decided he wanted to become an attorney. I remember he was diligent about attaining this lofty goal. He would work all day and attend law school at night in Stockton at Humphreys University, the Drivon School of Law. It was a really big deal in the company when he graduated. We were all so happy for him and attended the graduation ceremony and celebration afterwards. He opened his first law office in Modesto, L.F. Gianelli, and ran that for one year before he joined forces with Sidney Israels to form Gianelli & Israels.

Bud's three sons also eventually became attorneys; Mike Gianelli joined the Gianelli & Israels law firm in 1978 after working two years at Friedman and Rose, Jim Gianelli ran the Sonora law firm for 35 years, and Dave Gianelli joined what was then his father's Gianelli Mayol Siefkin & Brew law firm about 9 years after working in an accounting firm, and then at a law firm in Sacramento.

While Bud was still attending law school and working at Freese & Gianelli, Governor Wilson called me and asked if I'd like to become a probate referee helping clients with their estate by reviewing inventory and appraising the value. At that point I was serving in public office and had no inclination to add anything more to my roster. I told the Governor he should talk to my boss, that Bud was well educated and intelligent and was taking law classes, that he would be a perfect fit. Bud happily took the post.

He served in that position for 25 years and at one point became president of the State Referee Association. He also became well known as a champion for small business and helped to form thousands of businesses in this community.

On top of all of this, he was also a professional tennis referee, an avid scuba diver, ran several political campaigns and was active in many community organizations.

At the time Bud left Freese and Gianelli, he sold me his shares. By then Ogden Freese had passed away. Bob Stevens, who was a minor partner, decided he was going to sell his shares to me as well, so I wound up owning the balance of the firm.

I kept the name Freese and Gianelli for a long time until I had heart surgery, when I changed the name to the Simon Companies which just made more sense logistically. The Simon Companies at that time included Freese and Gianelli Claim Service, Status Bill Review, Status Medical Management, Status Investigations, and Simon and Simon Investments.

Bob Piccinini, founder of Save Mart Supermarkets and a good friend of mine for many years, called me one day and asked if I would take over his workers' compensation, that he had a huge workers' comp reserve and wanted to change companies. Well, we didn't do worker's compensation back then but I thought it would be good to add it to the Simon Companies, and decided to name this new division Pegasus.

I got the idea for the name from the Jamaica Pegasus Hotel, which impressed me when Joan and I stayed there. Greek mythology's flying horse, Pegasus, can mean limitless imagination, creativity, freedom and power. It's easy to see why I was enthralled with it.

Bob was a very successful local businessman and Save

Mart was the largest privately owned grocery chain in California. After Bob passed I learned from a very good friend of his that Bob would get all kinds of advice on how to run Save Mart, but would only trust his old friends in Modesto for advice. Apparently that practice paid off.

Our son Jeff inevitably ended up working in my firm. For many years one of the various things Pegasus Risk Management, our public entities claims unit, offered our employees and also community members outside of our corporation was classes for those who wanted to learn more about workers compensation administration and policies.

Jeff was interested in following his fathers' footsteps in law enforcement. He signed up to study at the Ray Simon Regional Criminal Justice Training Center, and took evening classes in reserve officer training at the academy. Jeff became a reserve deputy sheriff for about two years.

He had always been quite entrepreneurial and after college had started his own business in portable photo-copying. He would contact attorneys, doctors, and other businesses and take his portable equipment to their estab-lishment to copy whatever they were requesting.

An employee, Virginia Etcheverry, one day suggested we have Jeff come into this business. She knew him to be an enterprising young man and thought this might be the perfect setting for him, and it would benefit Pegasus as well. I invited him to come take the workers compensation course and he did, and he loved it – he was instinctively good at it. I was very happy to welcome Jeff into my corporation.

With our newborn son and feeling secure in my job, Joan and I decided to leave Hampshire Lane and build a new home, which we were very pleased with overall. Fortunately, I had been successful in my work and earning enough to furnish it, to our immense pleasure. Our first child, Jeff, was born in Memorial Hospital South near Modesto, in Ceres, California, which had been built in 1970.

On the day of Jeff's birth, I remember sitting and waiting a long time for Joan to finally have the baby. She was having a bit of a tough time because he was a large baby. When I got back to the hospital that evening to visit him in the newborn nursery, to look at him through the glass partition really, I couldn't find him. Panicked, I called out to the nurse and exclaimed, "I can't find my son."

She said, "You have to talk to the doctor," giving me further reason to panic.

When the doctor arrived, I said, "Where's my son?"

He said, "Come with me," and boy, my heart was beating so fast I thought I was going to faint. He brought me to this room, the newborn intensive care unit (now referred to as the Neonatal Intensive Care Unit, or NICU), and in this room was an incubator, and sticking his feet out the end was Jeff.

I said, "What's the matter with him?"

The doctor said, "He turned a little blue after birth

because it was a very hard birth for Joan. But don't worry, Ray, your son will be able to go home tomorrow."

Well, taking Jeff home was quite an experience. As any new parent can tell you, a newborn can be a handful, and thankfully Joan's parents Signe and Benny Pedego were able to help us quite a lot. We'd often take Jeff to their home so we could give the baby some time with his grandparents, and a respite for ourselves as well. They absolutely loved their new grandson, and it was a blessing for us as new parents to have this support.

We had a lot of fun with Jeff as a baby. Sometimes he was crying a lot; other times he was laughing. I use to get home from work when he was a toddler and find him jumping up and down on the sofa yelling "Daddy!" with his hair flying in the air.

As he grew older, he had a good friend who lived down the street named Doug Barham. He and Doug were inseparable. Jeff was kind of bossy with his friends, and he talked Doug into pulling him around in a wagon all the time.

After Jeff's fourth birthday, Joan and I talked about having another child and we were hoping to have a girl. On the night Joan was to give birth I took Jeff over to his Uncle Steve Pedego, Joan's brother, and returned to the hospital. I had no more than entered the hospital when I met Joan's obstetrician, Dr. Klor, as usual holding his cigar in his mouth.

He looked at me, smiled and said, "Guess what? You've got a girl." We grabbed each other's hands and danced around in a circle, both of us laughing. It was quite a scene. So now we had a boy and a girl and our family was complete.

Julie was a delight to raise. She was always quiet and wide eyed and forever wanted to be with her big brother Jeff. They took to each other like ducks to water. Every morning when Julie was a small baby, Jeff would hear her wake up and carry her out of her bed into the family room to turn the TV on. Joan and I would get up and find them both sitting on the sofa watching television, Jeff sitting with his arm around his baby sister.

She loved being a constant sidekick to Jeff and his buddy Doug. In those days the children could play outside all day and into the evening without fear.

Thankfully Julie enjoyed school and did very well, and she had many friends. We were always very happy for her. She took dance lessons with Lenore Hughes, Dance City, who had put together a fantastic ensemble of about 16 boys and girls into a synchronized ballroom dance group. The boys dressed in black tuxedos and the girls in flowing white gowns.

When they danced, they were simply dazzling and they performed around California in various venues. Joan and I were so proud of Julie that we would go anywhere they were performing. One year at the final performance they were invited to go to the World Ballroom Dance competition in Blackpool, England. Lenore called us for permission for Julie to go. When we took it up with Julie she emphatically said, "No, I won't go. I don't want to be away from here and my friends, period!"

I didn't understand why she didn't see it like we did

and was a little disappointed when she declined this once in a lifetime opportunity. To say the least, we were crushed, but we respected that she had her reasons for not going. I don't know if she ever regretted that decision. The dance group did go, and I believe her group came in 2nd in the world, and Lenore's Dance City dancers were invited to that competition in England, not once, but twice.

Julie was quite busy with school, dance, and other activities. Previously she had never had time to cultivate an interest in community service or joining clubs. At some point her mother's involvement in the Omega Nu Sorority seemed to resonate with her, and she joined in 2007. In 2021 Julie was elected president and $65,000 was raised for various charities during her post, in spite of this interval occurring during the coronavirus disease pandemic.

Eventually Julie met Greg Avery who was working with his dad, a building contractor constructing a subdivision they were developing. They got engaged and were married a year later, and still live in Modesto where Julie assists Greg managing their industrial park.

Jeff ultimately met his future wife, Tuesday Van Dyke when he was at Modesto's City Hospital working on photocopying documents for the hospital. Tuesday was working as a registered circulating nurse, as a patient advocate and performing nursing care for surgery candidates.

I n 1961 during the Cold War, President Kennedy encouraged citizens to build bomb shelters because of the possibility of nuclear fallout, in case the Soviet Union decided to attack. That same year Modesto built a new high school, Grace M Davis, its third high school after Modesto High (1918), and Thomas Downey High School (1951).

Following the theme of bomb shelters, architects designed this new project with very thick walls. I understand each wall was created by laying down heavy-duty sheets of plastic over large river rocks set in a frame, and pouring in a material, possibly cement. It hardened over the rocks which created an irregular, bumpy section of wall. You can still see those walls at Davis High – they aren't going anywhere!

One of our neighbors, Dave Bristow on Hampshire Lane, felt a great fear about the Russians possibly attacking and took President Kennedy's advice to heart. Dave was very intelligent and a really nice guy. He was a veterinarian and worked for the state; his title was veterinarian-in-charge at the Turlock CA Pathology Laboratory and was revered as California's poultry specialist pathologist.

He and his wife Diana feared this terrible warning might come to fruition, and were so concerned that Dave actually had a bomb shelter dug in his back yard. He came over one day and said, "Ray, if something happens, come over and bring Joan and your kids." I asked if I could see it, and followed Dave back to his home. We climbed the ladder down, and I found myself in a hole with moisture on the walls from the sprinklers above. It was the darkest, gloomiest place I'd ever seen. I told myself I'd take my chances with the nuclear fallout – there was no way I could bring my family to escape to a bomb shelter.

J oan very much enjoyed volunteer community service and joined a myriad of clubs in Modesto. She served in the capacity of President of Memorial Hospital Volunteers and also for the Friends of Community Hospice Foundation, Vice President Modesto Republican Women Federated, and Treasurer of McHenry Mansion Docents. She also belonged to Omega-Nu Sorority, the Women's Auxiliary of Memorial Hospital, Modesto's Community Hospice, and the McHenry Mansion.

If you drive through downtown Modesto, you will find a number of things named after Robert McHenry, including his private residence which is referred to as the McHenry Mansion and was designed in the High Victorian Italianate manner, completed in 1883, and the McHenry Museum (formerly McHenry Library) constructed with funds he designated for a library downtown which was finished in 1912 – six years after McHenry's death.

Another historical landmark built and owned by Robert McHenry, the Bald Eagle Ranch House on Crawford Road in Modesto sat on more than 4,000 acres of farmland and was built in the Late Victorian/Queen Ann style using mail order architectural plans. It was completed in

1893. McHenry Avenue runs from the south side of Modesto in the downtown area, to a little over nine miles north to the City of Escalon in San Joaquin County.

However, when you delve into Robert McHenry's history, you'll find Janet Lancaster's research reveals McHenry was actually a Civil War deserter named Robert Henry Brewster who found his way to Stockton, California and eventually Modesto around 1850. At the young age of 23, history shows he changed his name from Brewster, adding the prefix Mc to his middle name Henry, to form his new identity: Robert McHenry. Eventually he became known as one of Modesto's most distinguished leaders who had a great impact on this area.

As for myself, I joined the Junior Chamber of Commerce and was happy to make many friends there, and had the opportunity to volunteer for the City of Modesto as a planning commissioner. It was probably the worst job I ever had, although it led me to being on the Modesto City Council.

One of the city councilmen — Bud Patton who owned the Patton Vending Company — had passed away and left a vacancy. I decided to gather all my friends together and make a run for the seat. I walked door-to-door around almost the whole city — at least the voting city. I would push Julie in her stroller and Jeff would walk with his mother, and sometimes we would ride our bikes with Julie in a bike carrier seat sitting behind me. We passed out leaflets and won the first race by an overwhelming margin. This was going to open a whole new life to me and my family.

The mayor was Lee Davies, formally manager of the Pacific Telephone office in Modesto and he also had been a colonel in the Army. Dale Smith was a councilman and worked for the J.S. West Propane Gas company as a controller. Bill Hughes was a real estate developer. Jon Shasted was an executive vice president of E&J Gallo Winery overseeing all financial and legal matters. John Sutton was a shoe salesman; he and his wife later died in a terrible airplane crash in the Grand Canyon, leaving again another vacancy.

Later on, as people came and went from the city council, there were interruptions from the flow of republicans serving. One was Phil Newton, Modesto's first black city councilman, who worked for Knudsen's Dairy and the Stanislaus County Sheriff's Department as a correctional officer. Another was a schoolteacher named Jim Dixon. They voted against everything that ever happened on the city council and Mayor Davies was getting fed up with the constant bickering.

I decided to become a peacemaker, so after every council meeting I would ask these two men if they wanted to go for coffee, and they always did. During our coffee sessions, we seemed to get along well. They trusted me, and I trusted them. I gradually guided them in the procedures and methods of the city council, and eventually in council sessions we could have reasonable arguments and come to agreement, and I believe that's one reason why they ultimately made me Vice Mayor.

One major issue that seemed to affect the city was the question of establishing a new major shopping center on the Gagos property in northwest Modesto. George Gagos was a very good friend of mine, and he was selling the property to a major developer. It was to be a great money producer for our city, but downtown Modesto began to fade away as businesses moved into the vicinity of the new Vintage Faire Mall. Over a number of years, the downtown area actually became kind of a ghost town, as no new businesses would move into the old city center but rather out to the more modern mall area. Naturally this attracted even more new development near the mall.

D uring the second of my eight years on the City Council in 1968, my fifth divine intervention occurred. It happened in Los Angeles County, in Southern California.

Mayor Lee Davies was President of the National League of Cities. We both traveled by air to Disneyland, and I went to the council meetings available to me and he went to chair the presidential meetings. We stayed in the Disneyland Hotel in Anaheim, and outside the window of my room I watched the Disneyland helicopter take guests and fly off from the Disneyland Heliport to the Los Angeles International Airport and back.

On one of the meeting days, I talked to Lee and suggested we take the helicopter on the day we were to leave and fly to Los Angeles, then take United Airlines from Los Angeles, which would be a shorter trip for us. He agreed and said, "Go buy the tickets," which I did.

On the morning of August 14, I had my bags packed and walked down to the terminal, waiting for Lee to arrive to board the helicopter. Well, Lee was nowhere to be found, and I realized that the helicopter was about to take off. I ran into the building and found him giving a speech, which was about to conclude. At that point, I also heard the helicopter start up and fly off.

I was quite upset and told him I had just wasted eighty dollars. He said, "No, we'll pay you back. I'll try to find us a ride to the Orange County airport."

He found a councilman from Orange County to give us a ride, and we all got in his car. As we drove, for a while we could see the tail end of the helicopter in the distance moving through the sky towards Los Angeles. We had been driving for about fifty miles when we heard over the radio a news flash from KGO News that the helicopter from Disneyland had just crashed in the middle of Los Angeles County. The report was that three elected officials from Bakersfield and three from Fresno all died in the crash. In fact, a total of 21 were killed that day: 18 passengers and three crew members.

There was total silence in the car; no one talked. Lee looked at me and I looked at him, and we both had tears in our eyes. I blurted out, "You just saved my life and yours!"

He looked at me, and even though I know he was not a religious man, he said, "No, Ray. God saved our lives."

To me, it was my angels at work again — another divine intervention. It was happening time and time again to me. I was meant to go home and be with my wife and children.

Every time I met Lee Davies after that and had to introduce him at some meeting, I would always introduce him as the man who saved my life by being late!

Ray, Joan and Jeff as a toddler (1961)

Young Jeff Simon (1962)

Young Julie Simon (1971)

Ray with his daughter Julie at her wedding (1989)

Ray with his daughter Julie at her wedding (1989)

RAYMOND C. SIMON

Joan and Ray, 50th Wedding Anniversary (2007)

Simon Family, 50th Wedding Anniversary. Top Row L-R: Greg & Julie Avery, Ray, Tuesday and Jeff Simon, Corbin; Bottom Row L-R: Cameron Avery, Courtney Avery, Joan, Jessica & Dan Vella, Christian Simon (2007)

8

TRAVEL

Being on the City Council offered me many chances to travel. On one trip in particular, there was a National Association of Cities meeting in San Juan, Puerto Rico. We voted on the council to pay for four people to attend this meeting. Back then, Harry Kullijian was on the City Council, and so was Phil Newton. The three of us took the opportunity to travel to Puerto Rico to attend the conference together. It was the first time I had ever been out of California on a foreign trip as a councilman.

Besides serving on the Modesto City Council, Harry Kullijian may be best known for marrying his childhood sweetheart after a 70 year separation, the famous Broadway star/singer/dancer/comedienne Carol Channing. Carol wrote of their reuniting in her memoir: *Just Lucky I Guess*. Harry and Carol were a delightful couple and we became great friends.

On the first morning we woke up in San Juan we heard

marching in the street and crowds of people yelling, "Cuba, *si*; Yankee, *no!*" They were communists for Cuba, and certainly not for the US meetings there.

We were able to travel all over San Juan and out into the countryside, visiting the fort at the San Juan National Historical site, some wonderful restaurants, and part of Old San Juan that was really interesting. We were all invited to a doctor's home — almost the entire delegation from each state. He lived in a gigantic estate outside of San Juan. They had hors d'oeuvres, drinks, music, and dancing. It was quite a glorious event.

I recall the host standing at the door with his lovely, beautiful wife wearing a long flowing dress. Standing next to her was a magnificent-looking young woman, much younger, in a rather revealing dress. Both women were greeting all the guests as they came in. We became acquainted with one of the women from San Juan and I asked, "Is that his daughter?"

She replied, "No, that is his mistress, and she attends every event."

It became evident that most of the wealthy men in San Juan had a girlfriend in the city, with the knowledge of the wife. I told Joan that it was a rather clever thing, and she said, "Don't get any ideas! That won't happen here."

I also remember having wonderful sausages, and I couldn't get enough of them; they were absolutely delicious. A Puerto Rican woman walked up to Joan and said, "If I were you, I would tell my husband to cut back on the sausages. They are pure blood sausages that make stateside people very sick sooner or later." I decided I would not eat any more, but I never did get sick.

When the conference was over, we continued on to Jamaica with the Kullijians and Newtons. It was not far away, and as we knew some people in Jamaica it would be easy to travel there. The cook at the Sundial Restaurant in Modesto, Klaas Ooms, was married to a lady named Cindy who made all the arrangements for us even before we left Modesto. Mabel Cindy Hue Ooms had been born in Claredon, Jamaica, and her relatives were very well known in the capital city of Kingston.

Cindy Ooms had a sister, Winnie, who worked for the managing editor of the Modesto Bee, Ray Nish. Winnie's husband was a soldier of fortune and would go to fight wherever there was a revolution. I had the chance to meet him once; he really was a warrior.

When we arrived at the airport in Kingston it was around noon and the military had decided to shut the airport down for a couple of hours. We wandered around in the lobby until the newspaper people arrived who thought that some kind of official from England was there as I was being called Vice Mayor over the loudspeaker.

Sitting outside the airport in a limousine was Cindy's friend Percy Lee, a local celebrity and very wealthy man. We knew Percy was important when he walked into the airport and began arguing with officials to allow us to come out. He didn't want to wait any longer.

Finally, they released us, and photographers began shooting film of us on the way to the car. We were put up in the Pegasus Hotel, which was a magnificent structure in downtown Kingston. We were told that the following morning we were to meet the Mayor of Kingston, who was a friend of Percy Lee's.

That morning we were picked up again by limousine. When we arrived in downtown Kingston, there must've been ten thousand people lined up chanting, protesting over something in front of the Mayor's office. At each end of the line of chanting people were trucks filled with soldiers with machine guns pointed at the people.

We got out of the car and Joan went first towards the door between a line of people who grew suddenly silent. In fact, the whole group of people became silent: it was as if the Golden Goddess had arrived.

We entered the building and went to the mayor's office. He was a giant of a man. He was black and spoke with a very beautiful English accent. He showed us around City Hall and then introduced us to the city attorney and several other administrative officers. He then provided us with a beautiful lunch in a dining room that looked like it came right out of a palace in England.

That night we were invited to Percy Lee's house in what was called Beverly Hills — a group of magnificent mansions above Kingston. He had also invited the Mayor of Kingston and his next-door neighbor, Mr. Chang. As we were standing on Percy's patio prior to the dinner, we looked over at Mr. Chang's house, another resplendent residence with a large patio overlooking Kingston at night. What I saw startled me slightly: there were probably four men with automatic weapons patrolling the house. No one else seemed to think this was disturbing in the slightest.

Mr. Chang and the mayor arrived for dinner and we enjoyed a lovely Chinese meal. I learned during our repast that Percy was a General Electric distributor for the entire Caribbean, and that Mr. Chang owned every house of ill repute locally. Another friend, Cock Chicken, owned a bar of the same name and dealt in professional gambling where people, that is dignitaries and townspeople, could lay bets on playing bridge and professional boxing. It was a very beautiful dinner party with a lot of friendly, welcoming people.

Afterwards, we returned to our hotel. The next morning we went down to breakfast and saw that the *Daily Gleaner*, the local newspaper in Kingston, Jamaica founded in 1834, had a headline stating that the city attorney had been assassinated on his way home from work. He was the very man we had met in the Mayor's office the day before.

J oan and I decided we wanted to see the island, so we hired a driver at the hotel. I was curious about some people we had noticed in the city of Kingston who were dressed differently than anyone else we'd seen there, and they spoke to no one. They came in a group in a cart, and they left together in a cart. I learned later from the driver that these people were called Maroons and lived in the coffee country in the mountains.

It was a whole community of Jamaicans who had been there since the British occupied the island. They never allowed an outsider in their town and ran their own community government, and it was a very restrictive community. No one knew what really went on there. There were always well-intentioned people from Kingston and other cities in Jamaica who went there seeking information or tried to make contact, and they were turned away at the gates.

When I looked up their history, I found that the Jamaican Maroons were escaped slaves who had run away from Spanish plantations when the British took over in 1655. They formed independent communities in the mountainous areas as free men and women. The Maroons fought the British colonists and eventually freed themselves in 1739. Their land was given to them and they were to govern themselves. This occurred a full century before slavery was abolished in Jamaica in 1834.

Another interesting side note was that one of the friends of the Ooms's was a dressmaker with about a hundred people in her building making clothes to be shipped overseas. They made beautiful saris. Joan was taken down for a fitting for a custom-made dress and it was the most magnificent thing. And then they gave the dress to her! They would not let us pay for it.

With the driver, we traveled all over the island but in particular to the end of the island, which was a very ancient town built by Spain that looked like an old Spanish city. We went into the church, which was dated 1720, and saw many of the monuments built in the floor of the church reflecting prominent people in the community, dating back to the beginning of the church there.

I'm not certain how many of these people had seen white people like us. There was a group of about fifty who followed us all over the small town and had to frequently be ushered away from us by the driver, as they were constantly trying to touch us. The town was called Spanish Town, and there was a harbor that some of the historical notorious pirates (1690-1730) considered their safe haven. It looked much like the iconic Pirates of the Caribbean attraction at Disneyland.

When we returned to Kingston, we stopped by Cock Chicken's gambling hall because he had invited us to see his office. It was very modern and well furnished, with a number of big-screen televisions. While we were sitting there talking to him — he was a little guy, all dressed in white, white shoes, white hat, white coat, white pants, and a necklace — the phone rang, and we heard him say "Hello, Ezzard."

It was a conversation with Ezzard Charles who was coming to Kingston to participate in a world heavyweight boxing championship. He was known as The Cincinnati Cobra, the current heavyweight champion of the world. Little did we know that Cock Chicken was the sponsor, and in a week the championship was to take place in a downtown ring that he owned.

Ezzard Charles was famous for being the only man

who boxed the full 15 rounds with the great Joe Louis, aka The Brown Bomber, and win. He retired with a record of 95 wins, 25 losses, and one draw. He is the second greatest boxer of all time, behind Floyd Mayweather, Jr.

Cock Chicken was setting up a fight between Ezzard Charles and Sonny Liston. Needless to say, we were not able to stay for the fight, but we were impressed by the fact that he was a promoter of world-championship fights.

Our next-door neighbor in Modesto was a gentleman named Jack Veneman. He was a local farmer who ran for the State Assembly in Sacramento and won. I helped him a lot during that campaign, and we became good friends. He encouraged me throughout my career, and when Richard Nixon was elected 37th President of the United States (1969-1974), Nixon brought Jack back to Washington to serve as Assistant Secretary of Housing and Urban Development.

Joan and I, in fact, went back to Washington several times and were with the Venemans most of that time, touring Washington and learning all about Jack's job. Later on he changed jobs and went into the President's office as Director of Domestic Affairs. Another gentleman we knew through Jack was Robert Finch. He was previously Lieutenant Governor of California.

When we returned to Modesto after our trip to Puerto Rico and Jamaica, I learned that the vacancy created by Jack was going to be filled in an election. Jack was anxious for me to try to fill his job as the nominee of the republican party in Stanislaus County. I ran in the primary and was elected as the republican nominee. On the opposite side was a gentleman named Ernie Lacoste, a democrat. I got my first taste of statewide politics, and a lot of dirty tricks were pulled.

The republican party was raising a lot of money for me, and the democratic party was working hard for Lacoste. One day I got a call from Veneman who said he was in Sacramento and was going to stay at one of the motels with Bob Finch and several others who wanted to discuss with me how they were raising money for my election. I met Veneman in the lobby, and he took me to one of the rooms where Bob Finch was staying. When we arrived, Finch was sitting on a bed in his underwear and began talking to us about how he was going to raise money.

The telephone rang and I heard Finch say, "Yes, hello, Mr. President." It was President Richard Nixon, and Finch began telling Nixon why he was there and how he was raising money for Ray Simon. He turned on the speaker so that we could hear the President. That was probably a big mistake, because I have never heard such vile language coming from a President in all my life. They were talking about what was going on in Washington, and every other word from Nixon was a whole lot of expletives. Needless to say, when I left that room, I was in total shock.

Well, we had to campaign hard to win that assembly seat. However, it became impossible due to the high number of democrats living in the county. We won the City of Modesto easily but lost in South Stockton and the farming community. I thought it would be a big blow, but I just forged ahead after I lost until I realized that I didn't want to be on the council anymore, and it was up and out for me.

The next political objective that seemed obvious to me was to run for the Stanislaus County board of supervisors, District Seat 4. One of the members, Richard Vander Wall, a realtor in Modesto, was up for reelection for his fourth term. It was a major decision, but I decided I was going to run because I had won the City of Modesto in my bid for the assembly seat and felt certain I had the votes. Needless to say, Richard was not happy and came by to see me. He begged me not to run; he needed one more term to get his full retirement. I felt bad about it, but I would not change my mind. As soon the announcement was made I saw great support, not only from the newspapers but from friends of mine. We raised nearly $60,000 to campaign with, and I won.

Back then, approximately 65,000 people lived in District 4. By the time I left the board thirty-two years later, the population of this district was nearly 100,000. This was the greatest job I ever had as a part-time elected job. The pay was around $500 a month and there was only one meeting each month, and I had an office with a personal secretary. Little did I know that I was going to stay in this job for eight terms. I had an opponent nearly every time, and campaigned hard each election. I never took the job for granted.

While serving on the Stanislaus County board, I had many opportunities presented to me. One of the most interesting was establishing a relationship with a county in France in a process called twinning and it was an idea I gladly promoted. After World War II European countries started twinning, or pairing, towns (mostly between France, England, and Germany) in order to rebuild relationship with towns that were harmed in wartime.

The French put together a delegation to come to Modesto at our request, and when they arrived we are assigned them to individual homes. Joan and I were fortunate to host a French senator and his family. His name is Jean Arthuis, and his wife's name is Bridgette. They brought with them a delegation of mayors from this particular county Mayenne.

We took them everywhere in California — over to Monterey, San Francisco, and then up to our house at Lake Tahoe. They all spoke English and I tried to get by with the little French I knew. Something interesting I learned was that in France you can hold a number of offices that are political, whereas in the United States you can only hold one political office at a time. In fact, I learned that the French treat their politicians like royalty. Jean Arthuis was not only a senator but was also called Consiel General, which meant he was in charge of a number of cities in the County with a huge staff and a personal driver. On top of that he was Mayor of his small town, Château-Gontier.

The following year we took a delegation to France.

After arriving in Paris a group of us, all committee members of the Twinning Counties, traveled by bus to Mayenne and were invited to stay in the homes of different people in County Mayenne or Château-Gontier. Joan and I were invited to stay with Consiel General Arthuis in his small town of Chateau Gontier. He lived in a 130-year-old three-story home on about three acres. It was a beautiful place.

There were a number of social get-togethers to celebrate our presence in France. We were the honored guests at a large banquet sponsored by the French people and were invited to see the Grand Prix d'Amérique in Paris, which was quite exciting. We were rooting for one horse which belonged to someone from Mayenne; the horse was called Insert Gedde. In spite of all of us cheering for Insert Gedde, this particular racehorse came in third and we were all good-naturedly disappointed. We then returned to the Senator's home.

The following morning, a Sunday, he mentioned that he had to attend a function about 90 miles to the south and asked if I wanted to go along. It was going to be a ceremony for giving medals. In the small town that day was the Mayor, and I could swear it must have been General Charles de Gaulle's brother; the likeness was remarkable.

Arthuis kindly gave his speech partially in French and partly in English — the latter for my benefit. He said I was the first person this small town had seen who was American since the town was repatriated by American soldiers in 1945. That was a very meaningful and humbling event for me, being honored for the Americans who fought and died for France.

———

During the next several years on the Board we repeated this expedition three or four times, each countryman traveling back and forth. Each time we went, we all grew closer. On one trip back we were taken out into the countryside to a magnificent château that belonged to a cheese manufacturer. It was the largest milk and cheese company in France, and the gentleman who lived there was putting on a party for us, inviting a large number of people. I personally sat next to a lady who owned 130 grocery stores across France.

In the spring of 1990, the Senator called and asked if I would come to France and visit him and his family. It was an unusual request, and I asked if it was a special event. He said it was; that under President Jacques Chirac the Senator had been appointed Ministère de l'Economie et des Finances (Minister of Economy and Finance) and had been sworn in as such. He said, "You may bring a number of guests with you if you choose — maybe four people."

Not long after this conversation, I was in a restaurant having lunch when I overheard several people speaking French behind me. It was only a few days away from the celebration of the French Revolution and we had decided to host a small party at our house, decorating with French flags and inviting our Committee Members. I introduced myself and asked the lady who she was, and she said her name was Mme. Caroline Darbonne and that she lived in Paris.

Well, she came to our home and enjoyed meeting all of the Committee Members and our friends. I told her I had been invited to Paris to the Senator's home and office, as he had recently been sworn in as the new Ministère de l'Economie et des Finances and there was to be an official celebratory event. She asked if I would call on her when I arrived and see if she could come with us, as she had heard of Senator Arthuis and would very much like to meet him.

I asked George and Dianne Gagos and Jim and Bridget Mayol if they wanted to travel with us. They agreed, and shortly thereafter we flew to Paris. We were staying in the Hotel du Louvre. When I called the Senator's office and told him we had arrived, I was instructed that the next day the secret police would call on us for our identification. They said they would be at the bar in the Hotel du Louvre at six o'clock p.m.

We all gathered in the hotel bar at the appointed time, and shortly thereafter, we heard sirens. Pulling up in front of the hotel were four or five police cars with blue lights flashing and sirens blaring. Several gentlemen came into the bar and began checking our identity. Of course everyone in the bar turned to see what was going on.

The police escorted us to their automobiles and we headed for the Ministère de l'économie, des finances et de la relance (Ministry of Economy, Finance and Recovery), sirens shrieking their distinctive ee-oo-ee-oo all the way to a gigantic complex in the middle of Paris. It had a circular driveway in front, which we pulled into. We noticed that there were two gentlemen dressed in a livery coat and pantaloons. They were standing near a red carpet that had been rolled out from the building. It was quite impressive.

We walked into the building and took the elevator to the fifteenth floor, which happened to be the Senator's private living quarters there in the Ministry of Finance building. We were ushered into the dining room which had a long oak table, and in the door came the Senator — or now Ministère de l'Economie et des Finances — and his wife, Brigette. They greeted us all and I introduced Mrs. Darbonne, who he had agreed would be allowed to sit with us.

At that table were several ministers from other government sectors; Senator Arthuis had invited these gentlemen to attend the dinner as well. The meal was a feast. We were served by five or six waiters, with assorted wines for each course and a host of other delicacies. We had a wonderful time.

We learned that Mrs. Darbonne was a leading cookbook author in France, with 29 books to her credit to date. At the time we also believed that she was the owner of three restaurants, and co-owned another with Michelin Star Chef Guy Savoy. However, we did face the challenges that speaking different languages can bring to thoughtful communication, and were unsure if we had understood that information correctly.

Mrs. Darbonne's husband owned the Superb Herb company with offices all over the world. One of his offices is actually in Modesto, near Ceres.

To add a bit of humor to this story, as we left the Ministère de l'économie, des finances et de la relance, Mrs. Darbonne's car was parked across the street. She got into it and then it wouldn't start because the battery had run down. The next thing I knew, all of us — George, Dianne, Jim, Bridget, Joan and I, all dressed to the nines — started pushing the car to get it started. It was a sight to behold and we had a good laugh about it later.

The six of us stayed in Paris for another four or five days, one evening eating in Mrs. Darbonne's restaurant Les Bouquinistes, which is very well known globally. Of course we were delighted with our dinner.

Mrs. Darbonne suggested several other dining establishments during our stay, and we thoroughly enjoyed some of the finest meals we'd had in all of Europe. Following those recommendations, we made reservations one night at the Guy Savoy Restaurant, one of Chef Savoy's most famous. To our consternation, it was probably the most expensive restaurant, or at least close to the most expensive restaurant we'd ever dined in. The wine alone cost the six of us over two thousand dollars. The meal was another thousand dollars per couple. Needless to say, my credit card was at the max.

On another trip to Europe with George and Dianne we ate in a restaurant called La Café Cere just off the main avenue to the Arc de Triomphe. It was on the second floor of a building. We arrived and walked in, and when the elevator door opened there were at least four men dressed beautifully in tails — full evening dress — to bring us into the restaurant. It was a gorgeous place with a glass ceiling made of cut colored glass.

As we were sitting waiting to be attended, we noticed a beautiful tall blonde lady, at least six foot one, walking in the door with a gentleman who had on a painter's hat — that is, a sweeping portrait hat. He was wearing a red cape and was about five feet tall. They were taken to a table that had a cup filled with paint brushes instead of flowers. It was a fascinating sight.

When we got our food — which again was very expensive — I turned to the waiter and asked, "Who are those people?"

He turned to me and said, "We don't talk about our guests." He whipped around and started to walk away. After about three steps he came back, looked at me, and said, "He is an artist, but his hat is more famous than his paintings." We all had a good laugh over that.

———

In another year, we went back to France with George and Diane, and then traveled to Italy, where we toured Rome.

We drove the entire coast, staying in various hotels along the way and visiting villages and many restaurants. We had a magnificent time.

We also drove in Italy along the Amalfi Coast, again

exploring villages and restaurants. We decided to visit the Isle of Capri directly from our hotel. It was a trip across the water in a large boat packed with people.

We arrived in Capri and enjoyed our visit however, when we decided to go back the ferry was packed and it was very difficult to board. Joan grabbed my hand and pulled me on, and George did the same for Dianne. The boat was listing on the left side and we were worried that it was going to sink. The wind started blowing and the waves were coming up over the side. There were probably sixty to eighty people on that little ferry boat, but we finally made it.

We drove on to Florence, Italy — which once again was a beautiful and interesting experience. One morning we were walking down the main street when we observed a beautiful building that looked like a hotel but was a restaurant. George had no fear of walking in, even though it was closed for business at that moment. The door was open, and he found a woman in the kitchen and asked if they served dinner on Sunday or Monday. She said, "You can come back on Monday, and it will be open."

We came back to the restaurant — Ristorante Enoteca Pinchiorri — on Monday and were led to a lovely table by the lady George had met in the kitchen. We soon realized she was the owner, and her name is Annie Féolde.

It turns out that Annie is one of the most famous chefs in the world, recognized as the very first female chef in Italy to win and hold three Michelin stars at her restaurant, and only the fourth female chef ever to be awarded that commendation. Annie told us she was to be honored in the United States in May, and asked if we would come. Unfortunately we could not at that time, and I'm not certain why. We were happy to have made a delightful new friend, and to know we were keeping such fine company. George always did have a nose for the finest restaurants.

As George and Dianne traveled with us across Italy, last on our itinerary was Milan as we were going to depart from the Milan Malpensa Airport for our return flight.

I had the habit of phoning my secretary Sandy Hopp every morning when traveling and while in Europe I'd let her know where we would be each day. She had told me the night before that an Italian gentleman was trying to get ahold of me, and that he was phoning from Milan; he wanted to set up a meeting in Modesto. I told Sandy to have him call me, and to let him know I happened to be in Milan. That is how I first met Alex Bonecchi.

Alex called in the morning and introduced himself, and said that his father, Dr. Alfonso Bonecchi, a mechanical and electrical engineer, wanted to meet with me. They were interested in looking at property in Stanislaus County and he understood that is where we are from.

He mentioned that his family were planning to be at their summer home to close it for the winter, and would we like to join them there so we could talk. That sounded intriguing and like it might just add to our already eventful vacation. Alex picked all of us up from our hotel and we made the beautiful drive with him to their villa.

In the course of our drive Alex explained that the Bonecchis were planning to travel to Modesto in the next few months to investigate building a new plant for the chemical extraction of tartaric acid from grapes. I learned that they had been trying to track me down so I might give them a clue as to how to start.

Tartaric acid, known generally as cream of tartar, is an organic acid that takes place innately in fruits in the process of fermentation, particularly in extraction from grapes or wine byproducts. Alex explained that they have these particular grape extraction plants all over the world wherever there are grapes, but not in Modesto where there are frankly quite a lot of grapes. I told him that by chance we were traveling with our good friend George, who was the best person to tell him about property.

George informed Alex that there was a place he should look into in South Modesto that might suit their needs, "There's transportation nearby, and many very small manufacturing plants."

Alex drove us to Lake Como and as we neared the Bonecchi estate, my vision until that point was of a small cabin on the lake. As we rounded a curve, I saw a huge home on the right surrounded by a parklike setting with an impressive fence. Alex pressed a button on the dash-board and the gates opened to a gigantic mansion.

We pulled into the driveway and much to our delight, walked into the most beautiful villa I had ever seen. It was actually a ninety-room palace owned at one time by

Emperor Maximilian and Carlota and it still had almost all the original furniture. This was the Bonecchis' "summer home."

Dr. and Mrs. Bonecchi and their two other sons were waiting to greet us as we arrived, and guided us indoors. We saw magnificent ancient tapestries on the wall, beautiful silver, two dining rooms, a ballroom with a balcony for the orchestra, a wine cellar in the basement, and sixteen bedrooms.

Later that day on our way back to Milan from the Bonecchis' beautiful home, we all had a good laugh as to what we had thought a summer home should be.

A year later I got another call from Alex who told me they'd found property from George's recommendations, and that engineers would be coming to build the plant. He asked if we would be coming to Europe this year, and I told him that yes, Joan and I had planned a vacation to Paris. He told me his parents wanted me to fly to Milan and be their guests at their summer home again, this time for about a week. We decided to fly to Milan before Paris, and Dr. Bonecchi and his son Geraldo picked us up at the airport. Dr. Bonecchi spoke broken English, whereas Geraldo spoke fluently and translated for most of our trip.

As a member of the Stanislaus County Board Supervisors, one issue I have is that whenever I accept an invitation, I insist on paying my way; paying for our dinners, or whatever it might be. Dr. Bonecchi was quite upset at this and he said it was really against Italian etiquette. After dinner I asked him, "Dr. Bonecchi, what's my portion of the dinner check?" I tried to explain that I have to pay for myself – I cannot accept what could be considered a bribe, and did he want me to go to jail because that is what would happen if I did. He acquiesced but was not happy about it. He said that was a terribly unacceptable practice in his presence.

Often, we'd eat in their home instead of going out. I remember Dr. Bonecchi wanted me to be Italian in the worst way. He even revised my name to Raimondo Simone. He'd try to teach me as much of their language and customs as possible; I think it was a goal he'd set for himself to convert me. Once, I remember a dessert was being served and he asked, "Vuoi panna liquida o panna montata?" I told him absolutely the panna montata — whipped cream, instead of liquid cream. When in Rome, do as the Romans do…

T he next summer Dr. Bonecchi, his wife Maria Pia who Joan had become friends with, and their son Alex came to Modesto as they were beginning to build the chemical plant with clients in Modesto and also a collection point for grape leaves from which the tartaric acid would come. They could make cream of tartar with it. Alex was twenty-seven years old, and very skilled as a chemist. He would be in charge of the Modesto plant.

As an interesting aside, my wife Joan is infinitely pleased with her matchmaking skills having introduced Alex to his future bride, the beautiful, intelligent, gregarious Dana Bosio. Dana is the daughter of our good friends who Joan had gone to school with, Dick and Angie Bosio.

Joan had gotten to know Dana quite well through a fundraising committee they were on together, and found her to be a delightful, kind, selfless, and hardworking young woman. When Mrs. Bonecchi came to Modesto to set up a home for Alex, she asked Joan for help, because she didn't speak English and did not know the area; she didn't know where to start.

Joan knew several friends who spoke Italian, but immediately thought of Dana who she knew was fluent. Dana's job at that time took her to Milan several times a year to organize business exhibitions. The matchmaker in Joan believed Dana and Alex would be perfect together.

First she introduced Dana to Mrs. Bonecchi, and naturally they hit it off very well, and Alex then met Dana through his mother. Dana helped them set up the household for Alex.

At first, Dana and Alex didn't seem to hit it off very well and Joan thought she had made a big mistake. But they started getting to know each other and then before we knew it they were getting married.

Dana still thanks Joan for that introduction, but Joan very happily just feels it was meant to be.

The family had a number of other types of plants in Milan. One of the sons managed a plastics factory, which made thin plastic film used in wrapping and had other uses, and this was to be distributed all over Europe and in some parts of America. The other son was in charge of a factory that made custom fabrics used by the couture houses. Many of the most famous dressmakers come from Italy, and many of them use Dr. Bonecchi's famous silk manufacturing plant.

We had several dinners for them at our home with other distinguished guests, and took them to a number of different places to visit. Even though they spoke little English and we certainly spoke no Italian, Alex could interpret well enough for us, and we got along fine. They made arrangements for us to come to Italy again in a couple of months to their home on Lake Como and stay for a couple of weeks.

We thought this sounded like a great opportunity and we planned our vacation. We flew to Milan where Dr. Bonecchi picked us up and drove us to Bellagio on Lake Como and their home.

When we went inside the palace, we were taken upstairs by a housekeeper. By the way, at that home, there were five gardeners, three chefs, a doorman, and five or six maids. The home had eleven bedrooms with an equal number of baths. The bedrooms were not just a bedroom with a bed and nightstands — each had a dining room, a living room, two baths, and a sunroom. Our bedroom had grand doors that opened out onto a balcony; we were on the third floor and opened the door in the middle of the night to look out at not one lake but three.

The first night we had dinner cooked by their chef in the "small" dining room, which had a table fifteen feet long with eight chairs. There were numerous beautiful tapestries on the walls, and in addition to that, a number of oil paintings of influential people from the 1700s. The room had an elegant crystal chandelier that would put any other I've seen to shame, and we enjoyed a wonderful five-course meal. The wine came from the basement, and that was a story in itself.

The doctor asked if I wanted to go to the wine cellar with him. We navigated our way down steep narrow concrete steps deep into the concrete cellar, which was very dark. He pulled a key out of his pocket that was probably six inches long — an antique bit or barrel key. He slipped it into the keyhole of a wooden door which creaked open, and he turned on the lights. At that point I could see shelf after shelf of wine bottles with dust covering them. It looked like something you'd see in a movie.

He walked by each wine shelf, turning bottles as he went, and asked me if I favored heavy or light red wine for dinner. I told him I preferred a light red wine. He pulled a bottle out; the name I don't know, but the label read 1923. I couldn't believe my eyes. We went upstairs and of course had the wine with dinner, and I will tell you, I have never tasted such smooth sweet wine as I did that night. Our dinner was a leg of lamb with small red potatoes, a salad, green beans, and spumoni for dessert.

We then retired to the living room where we conversed through interpreters, having a good time with all. The next morning they gave us a tour of the entire home. It was unbelievable to see the chapel; it had a magnificent altar of white gold, very ornate, with a beautiful stained-glass window behind it. It looked like one of the famous French chapels we had visited, only this one was small, seating twenty-five to thirty people. There were a number of stained-glass windows on the side. It simply was exquisitely ornate.

Next we went to the ballroom which had its own balcony for the orchestra, a hardwood floor for dancing, and padded seats on the side. It could probably hold about a hundred dancers, it was so large. There was another billiard room with pool tables, billiard racks, and pool cues, with a bar at one end that could not only serve mixed drinks but had several fountains for beer.

There was a library full of books and comfortable nooks for reading, and all the walls were covered with taxidermy-mounted wild animal heads and a hunting rack of guns on one side. The ceiling was painted much like the Sistine Chapel, with hand-painted angels and religious pictures all in color — a magnificent sight.

In the hallway leading to the front door was the actual historical sedan chair — the type of coach that would be carried by four chairmen — for transporting Empress Carlota through the streets of the city. The chair was covered with beautiful silk tapestry and elaborately decorated. This was the very sedan chair that essentially carried Maximilian and Empress Carlota.

I had taken an art history class at junior college and I knew the huge oil painting on the wall, about three feet by eight feet, to be a Rubens, which he confirmed.

I asked the Dr. if the furniture and artwork was from

the original palace and also how he had come about obtaining it. He said that his father had acquired it. Now, he was himself eighty years old, and so I asked, "In what year did your father purchase it?"

He revealed that his father had purchased the estate in 1923 during the Italian Revolution.

Dr. Bonecchi relayed a story of when he was a young boy sitting in the palace during the spring when he heard shouts and the firing of guns across the lake as he observed a number of cars racing down the highway; it was 1945. He watched as people pulled a man out of a car and put him in one of the other cars and drove off.

It was later that he learned, "It was the Partisans grabbing Benito Mussolini, Italy's Prime Minister, as he was trying to escape Italy, fleeing to Germany. They took Mussolini to the small village of Giulino de Mezzegra, to a gas station. They then hung him upside down by his heels, shot him, and left him hanging there for days. His girlfriend, who was with him, met the same dreadful fate."

On another evening the Doctor said, "We are going to Venice to the Danieli Hotel and partake in a formal dinner on the top floor overlooking the large waterway to Venice." That evening there was a boat parade, and all the boats were decorated with colorful lights. We watched as perhaps two or three hundred of them passed by. It was such a fancy affair that when Joan saw what Mrs. Bonecchi was going to wear, she had to begin shopping for an elegant dress to match.

When we went to the dinner, there were probably two hundred people sitting at long tables, all very stylishly dressed. The people next to us were speaking Spanish, so it appeared there were people from all over the world. During the course of the evening I turned to Mrs. Bonecchi and asked, "Where are these people from, and what do they do?" I was always curious about these kinds of things.

· She looked at me and said, "Petrol," which meant oil. These were obviously owners of the oil wells in Brazil.

Besides the lovely meals served in their home and the magnificent events we attended as their guests on Lake Como, we also investigated some local restaurants. One of the finest eateries we enjoyed was Villa d'Este Restaurant.

We learned that the Bonecchis boast some very distinguished neighbors, including Virgin Atlantic Airways' Richard Branson, and also actor George Clooney who owns Ristorante il Gatto Nero on Lake Como.

Ray and Joan, trip to Jamaica: Ray representing
Modesto as Vice Mayor, visiting the Mayor of
Kingston. Arriving at Norman Manley International
Airport in Jamaica's capital city of Kingston
(1972)

Joan's Parents: Ben and Signe Pedego (1975)

Ray and Joan, Roaring 20s Costume Party (1975)

Joan and Senator Jean Arthuis in Paris. Jean Arthuis had three
titles: Senator representing Mayenne in the French
Parliament, Ministère de l'Economie et des Finances and
Conseil General (1987)

Ray's first trip to Paris as a Stanislaus County Supervisor

Ministre des Finances Jean Arthuis with Ray at Arthuis'
apartment in Paris

Dining at the Paris apartment of Jean Arthuis, Ministre des
Finances. L-R: Brigette Arthuis, Joan Simon, Dianne Gagos,
John Arthuis, wife of the CEO, Arthuis' CEO, and George
Gagos

Arc de Triomphe, Paris, France

L-R: Jim and Bridget Mayol, Joan Simon, Jean Arthuis, George
and Dianne Gagos. Dinner at the apartment of Jean Arthuis,
Ministère de l'Economie et des Finances

Meeting with Senator Jean Arthuis and Senator Ballieau.
French Parliament Senate and National Assembly inside the
Luxembourg Palace in Paris

Ray at the Podium. French Parliament Senate and National
Assembly inside the Luxembourg Palace in Paris

Joan sitting in Napoleon Bonaparte's Chair. French
Parliament Senate and National Assembly inside the
Luxembourg Palace in Paris

Ray, Joan, French Senator Ballieau and his secretary, Monique,
Dianne and George Gagos. Trip to Paris inside the Luxembourg
Palace

Dec, 31, 2021

JEAN ARTHUIS

Dear Ray and Joan,

Brigitte joins me to thank you for your season's greetings. We are pleased to know that your health is good and vaccinated to prevent Covid. We are hopefully in the same situation, expecting the end of the pandemic.

We look forward to walk with Angels. No doubt, your biography will express a grand destiny mainly devoted to public interest, a significant example to youngsters.

We wish you a new year filled with love, happiness, health and editorial success.

Yours sincerely —

Jean & Brigitte

Letter from Jean Arthuis, Ministère de l'Economie et des Finances (2022)

Joan Simon, Ray Simon, Dianne and George Gagos. Chef Anna Féolde is the owner of Ristorante Enoteca Pinchiorri, in Florence, Italy

Bonnechi Summer Home, back side of home

Bonnechi Summer Home, back yard

Bonnechi Summer Home, back yard

9

PUBLIC AND COMMUNITY SERVICE

When we returned home and I went back to work at the Stanislaus County board of supervisors, I found out that the new Stanislaus County Sheriff's Department Regional Training Division, host to the Sheriff's basic academy and advanced officer courses, had been named after me. It was to be a training center for all Central California law-enforcement officers from various cities and counties throughout the State.

On March 10, 1988 I was honored at the County's dedication of the Ray Simon Regional Criminal Justice Training Center at the academy grounds on Crows Landing Road in Modesto. My wife Joan, our son Jeff Simon and his wife Tuesday, and my daughter Julie Simon Avery and her husband Greg attended with our grandchildren Jessica Simon, Christian Simon, Cameron Avery and Courtney Avery.

Supervisor Nick Blom, Chairman of the Stanislaus

County board of supervisors gave a brief speech as to the foundation of the Board's rationale for naming the Center after me. This ceremony was held prior to the public entering the Center's gym for the formal presentation, which was attended by about 200 citizens and dignitaries.

Making formal presentations were United States Federal Judge Frank Damrell, Jr., a Modesto native who had acted as a deputy in the Office of the State Attorney General of California (1964-1966), and a deputy district attorney of the Office of the District Attorney, California (1966-1968); and Dan Lungren, elected to Congress (1979-1989), the 29th Attorney General of California (1991-1999), and again to Congress (2005-2013). Dan was a powerful motivator of public safety tactics, including "Three Strikes," the Sex Offender Registry, and "Megan's Law." As you can imagine, I felt very privileged to have them both there to honor me.

My longtime friend the Honorable Frank Damrell, Jr. pronounced, "The Federal Court is dark this afternoon, in honor of Ray Simon."

The Honorable Dan Lungren stated, "The Training Center is the first and last bastion of individual freedoms and I am proud that Ray played such an extensive part on the California Board of State and Community Corrections to make this happen."

Afterwards, I was surprised, as were my fellow associates on the Stanislaus County Board of Supervisors, during a board meeting when Sheriff Lynn Wood approached the dais and exclaimed, "I'm going to make

Ray a deputy sheriff." Everyone was puzzled, and the County's counsel asked, "What do you mean?"

The Sheriff explained, "Under California law, I have the power of posse comitatus, which means that as Sheriff I am allowed to appoint anyone in the world to become a deputy sheriff, and I have made the decision to appoint Ray and honor him with a Stanislaus County sheriff's deputy badge.

"While Ray served on the Board of Corrections he encouraged the building of Stanislaus County's much needed new jail, and he served on the committee that determined to build criminal justice training academies state-wide. Ray has surpassed what we could ever have expected or hoped for in support of law enforcement, and especially our sheriff's department."

I was especially grateful that over the years I had spent a great deal of my free time serving on various criminal justice committees in the State. I know now that I was blessed with these honors because I had worked hard from the moment my path was clear to me, and I stuck to that path throughout my personal life and career.

From 1969 through 1974 I served at the pleasure of Ronald Reagan, then Governor of California, on the California Council on Criminal Justice. In 1972 I acted as the Regional Criminal Planning Board Chairman for Region K, which was our region, and then from 1979 to 1980 as Chairman of the Stanislaus-Area Association of Governments in regard to Criminal Justice. Governor George Deukmejian appointed me from 1985 through 1994 to the California Council on Emergency Services, and from 1992 to 1993 I was appointed by the Board of Corrections as Executive Steering Committee Member to revise California's local detention facilities.

My biggest appointment came in 1995 when I served Governor Wilson until 1999 as a Member of the California Board of Corrections. In 1998 to 1999 they called me back after I had retired and appointed me Chairman of the Executive Steering Committee for the Federal Violent Offenders program. I pretty well knew the criminal justice system, and we reorganized it from bottom to top.

At the state level, we found out that the prisoners were eating three hot meals a day, even steak. We changed the lunches to peanut butter and jelly and other small sandwiches; a normal lunch for many people, and some days we provided a hearty soup. It cost the State budget about $2.5 million to provide just one prison with a hot lunch over the course of a year, and there were fifteen to twenty prisons in California. We gave them a good breakfast and we gave them a good dinner, but we replaced the hot lunch with a still satisfying meal; it just wasn't extravagant.

The next thing we learned was that the prisoners were becoming stronger and more muscular than the guards. Placed in every single prison gym were hundreds of pieces of expensive weightlifting equipment, and the prisoners had the opportunity to spend quite a lot of their free time buffing up.

Naturally, there were riots in some of the prisons when we removed the equipment, but these were quickly subdued. The prisoners got used to the fact that they could no longer do that type of exercise.

The last five years of my term on the county board were probably the most productive of my entire political career. Most of my success can be directly attributed to Chief Executive Officer Reagan Wilson. He was brilliant in financing and planning. Whenever I came up with a constructive idea, that man put it into effect and made it a success, along with Patty Hill Thomas, who was in charge of construction and engineering.

One of those ideas was that we should combine City and County general offices in downtown Modesto to begin a renaissance of the downtown area. After months of meetings, we planned on 1010 Tenth Street to be the headquarters for both the city and county in the same five-story building. That would mean tearing down the whole block of buildings on J Street between 10th and 11th Streets, including two old dilapidated hotels, the Hotel Covell and Hotel Hughson which were both at one time considered cornerstones of downtown Modesto. This new headquarters was basically to become a one-stop shop for both city and county business.

After situating Mayor Lang and his staff on one half of the fifth floor and the county CEO Reagan Wilson and his staff on the other, we combined all departments for city and county; visitors could conveniently drive into one multi-level parking structure and visit both entities. It was a major construction project and wholly began the initiative of reviving downtown Modesto. A year earlier, you could have driven downtown over the weekend on Ninth Street, Tenth Street, all the way to Fifteenth Street, and G through M Streets and not see a person or a car.

We realized that having the Sheriff's Office in downtown Modesto was not to the advantage of the county. We owned a large parcel of land just outside of Modesto on Crows Landing Road, and since I was serving on the Board of Corrections at the time, I knew there was a lot of money available through the corrections board to construct new jails and administrative offices. Immediately I got our staffs together to plan on both. Over the next year we succeeded in constructing a new modernized jail and moving the sheriff's administrative officers out to that area.

We also began examining the effectiveness of the Stanislaus County Hospital which at that point was a mammoth building with around five hundred employees. We decided to outsource our hospital care of the indigent and got bids from all major health corporations. We ultimately settled on National Medical Enterprise, which was already operating Doctors Hospital in Modesto. We closed the county hospital and saved millions of dollars in exchange for more sophisticated medical care.

After our construction was completed at 1010 Tenth Street, all the surrounding vacant buildings began filling up and people started coming back downtown, slowly but surely. My friend Frank Damrell who at that time had his law firm Damrell, Nelson, Schrimp, Pallios & Silva, Attorneys, called me up one day and said, "I want to have a meeting with you, the Mayor, my sister, and a few others." His sister was Marie Gallo, married to Bob Gallo of Gallo Winery.

He continued, "My intention is to complete I Street into the main thoroughfare through Modesto. Marie wants to build a new Performing Arts Center, and the purpose of this meeting is to plan, because she can raise millions of dollars from her own family. We think we'll need a large piece of property on I Street that belongs to the county."

Since I was Chairman of the Board it was going to require a lot of work on my part to try to convince the other Board Members to donate the property and then help in the construction of the building. We began planning and approximately one year later we had all of the architectural designs and we were ready to move forward, as long as we could get the County's permission. So far, I only had one other person with me from the Board; Nick Blom and Tom Mayfield were strictly against it, and I needed all five votes before I could go ahead.

I determined that over the next few months I would give Nick and Tom all the votes they needed for all of their inconsequential projects. I did so, and in another six months when the vote came around for the County to donate the property and spend up to $2 million of general funds in the construction of the Arts Center, they went along. Gallo had come up with an offer of $5 million, and Marie Gallo set about raising private funds from everyone she knew. Before we knew it, we had $10 to $15 million for construction.

The building project went ahead, and it turned into a magnificent performing arts center on I Street. According to outside experts, it was the epitome of a performing arts center with one of the best sound systems in the world. In fact, one of the first shows when the Gallo Center for the Arts opened in September of 2007 boasted none other than Tony Bennett. He claimed the acoustics were the best he'd ever performed in, and to the delight of the audience he put down his microphone to sing the entire concert unaided.

We had initially hired the first director whose expertise was in construction. We then hired a new director, Lynn Dickerson, former editor of the Modesto Bee, for her management skills. She was extremely knowledgeable and capable, had good executive abilities, and was common sense savvy. She was able to move ahead with a Board of Directors that made this building and the performances a thing of majesty. It became a tremendous success, and through fundraisers, donations, and world-class productions, they took the debt down to only $2 million within 10 years.

The side benefit to this building was that hundreds of businesses small and large began to form around it. It was truly the final big step in the revitalization of downtown

Modesto. We needed a parking structure for this building, and further east on I Street was a lot that we could co-develop with a plan utilizing the majority of the five-story structure for parking and the balance as a private structure to move the District Attorney's office into.

I n 1972 Dr. Les Knowles called me and introduced himself as the Boys Advisor at Modesto Junior College. He asked if I could possibly form a foundation for MJC to help the underprivileged for scholarships and to buy books and other necessities for attending college.

I agreed, but told him I would need legal help and thought Jack Griffin, a local attorney, could help me.

Jack and I got together and prepared the legal documents. To register with the secretary of state to start a nonprofit, we first had to deposit some money into the account, so we both put up $100. We then formed a foundation committee. The first members included Henry Laws, Bette Belle Smith, Leonard Barlett, Marianne Bradford, Lowell Clark, Betty Schroder, Matthew Fiscalini, and Dr. Ronald Julien. Henry organized a number of meetings and over the next three to four years our account grew to several thousand dollars.

In 2001 there was a Foundation celebration with George Boodrookas, MJC's Dean of Advancement and Executive Director of the Foundation; the committee members and I attended as guests. George reported the foundation had a balance in that fund of $17,000,000 (seventeen million dollars). To think we started with just a couple hundred dollars. That was a very proud moment for me.

Because of my career and political appointments I have had the great fortune of meeting many famous people. Carol Channing, of course because she became our neighbor when she married our good friend Harry Kullijian; British singer Engelbert Humperdinck; Actress/singer Debbie Reynolds; Sonny Bono, well known for his singing career with Cher – their biggest hit was "I Got You Babe" – but he also got into politics later on in life. Joan and I were asked to host a fundraiser in our back yard for Sonny when he ran for Congress.

My good friend Dr. Mike (Archie) Kline, a local boy who became a beloved veterinarian in Modesto, and I were co-chair for the March of Dimes. One of the things we were tasked with was to walk door to door and ask for money. It might have been tedious alone, but with Mike Kline you'd never be bored.

We walked a good portion of Modesto, from the richest to the poorest neighborhoods. Our attitude was that every penny counts and contributing to a cause like this can be very self-fulfilling. We didn't want to assume that some areas may not want to be a part of it.

What we found surprised us very much. The poorest

neighborhoods, those in the south side of Modesto, gave the most. They were unflinching in donating to this great cause. We appreciated and were astonished at the response we received.

Because of our significant fundraising work with the Modesto March of Dimes, Mike and I were recognized as their biggest fundraising collectors in this time period. For this reason, we were offered the incredible opportunity to meet the world-renowned Dr. Jonas Salk, and invited for a personal tour of the brand-new Salk Institute for Biological Studies in La Jolla, California, where he was working on a cure for infantile paralysis. The building was interesting in that all of the scientists' offices had huge picture windows that faced the ocean. He told us it was common practice for each scientist to go to their office after lunch and lie down on a cot, facing the ocean. It was a time of contemplation.

He relayed an interesting story to Mike and me. "I was lying on my side on my cot, looking out the window of my room, mesmerized by the ocean waves and tides' ebb and flow, when the idea struck me of the vaccine technique that eventually worked."

Dr. Salk had developed the techniques that led to the vaccine to cure Polio, however he refused to ask for a patent for the Polio vaccine so that it could be better promoted worldwide. He spent the last years of his life working on an AIDS vaccine.

I met several Governors of California including Governor Ronald Reagan (1967-1975) before he became the 40th President of the United States; Governor George Deukmejian (1983-1991) who became a good friend, and

Governor Pete Wilson (1991-1999); Secretary of State Colin Powell (2001-2005); Dr. Marvalene Hughes, President of California State University, Stanislaus (1994-2005); California State Senator Jeff Denham (1988-2000); and Former US Speaker of the House of Representative Paul Ryan (2015-2019).

In 2010 at the home of Al and Kimberly Spina, Joan and I met Condoleezza Rice, the 66th US Secretary of State under George W. Bush and 8th Director of the Hoover Institution. Condi graciously appeared at the event as a concert pianist and not as a politician, to help raise funds for a non-profit (the Salida Performing Arts Foundation in partnership with the Classics for Kids Foundation) that provided an all-inclusion string immersion program, including over 100 violins, and a strings specialist teacher, to students at Sisk Elementary in the Salida Union School District for free.

Joan and I were invited to a fundraiser for George W. Bush, 43rd President of the United States, at Alex Spanos' home in Stockton. We visited with George and Laura Bush and found them very down to earth and charming company. The event happened to be in November, and I mentioned during our conversation that Joan's birthday was a few days away. Joan was surprised and delighted to receive a birthday card from Laura and George in the mail a few days later. They had remembered our conversation, and that it was Joan's birthday. We thought that was very thoughtful and gracious of them.

They kindly remembered me again when I retired from the Stanislaus County Board of Supervisors; I received a letter of accolades and congratulations from President George W. and Mrs. Bush.

———

One of the most entertaining incidents of my life happened in New York. Joan and I had gone to attend the Monty Python Comedy Troupe's musical comedy *Spamalot* when one of the actors singled me out.

He walked down to the seating area and asked my name in front of everyone and for some reason I thought it would be fun to say "Ramone Simone," and so I did. When I was a kid my brothers used to call me "Ol' Ramone Simone," I guess because they thought it was funny and it rhymed. Joan's mouth dropped open; she looked at me and exclaimed "What's wrong with you?"

The actor then invited me to go on stage with him during the show, and the cast surprised me by inserting my name into the song, *Lady of the Lake.* They sang "As long as your name is not Ramone Simone..."

The group then honored me with the Arthur Award: *Best Peasant – Monty Python's Spamalot.* I was shaken being up on that stage and it was a little embarrassing to be in the limelight at the time, but also a fun memory to look back on.

Ray with Governor Ronald Reagan (1969)

At a local fundraiser with Ronald Reagan. (May, 1969)

Ray on a campaign bike ride with Jeff, Joan, and Julie (February 1969)

Governor George Deukmejian appointing Ray to the
State Emergency Board (1986)

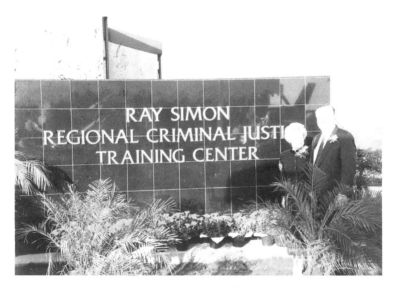

Ray and Joan at the Grand Opening of the Ray Simon Regional
Criminal Justice Training Center (1988)

Supv. Tom Mayfield, Ray, Grandchildren Courtney,
Christian, Jessica, Cameron, and Supv. Nick
Blom. Grand Opening of the Ray Simon Regional
Criminal Justice Training Center (1988)

Governor Pete Wilson, Joan and Ray at his appointment to the
California Board of Corrections (1995)

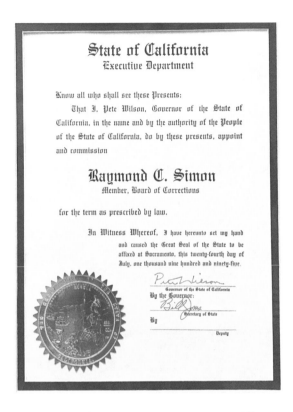

Certificate: Governor Pete Wilson appointed Ray
Simon to the California Board of Corrections
(1995)

Sonny Bono and a lady from the Republican
Central Committee, Joan and Ray (1997)

Ray meeting General Colin Powell with Marvalene Hughes of
California State University Stanislaus (1998)

Ray and Joan with Condoleezza Rice, 66th US
Secretary of State and Director of the Hoover
Institution, at the home of Al and Kimberly Spina

Harry Kullijian with his new bride, Carol Channing
(Hello Dolly), with Joan and Ray (2003)

Joan and Ray with Debbie Reynolds in Palm
Desert (2010)

Engelbert Humperdinck with Ray and Joan at the
Gallo Center for the Arts (2019)

Monty Python's Spamalot cast, New York, NY. Ray is
in the top row, fourth from the left (2004)

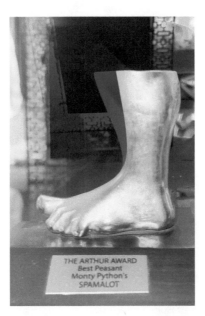

The Arthur Award, Best Peasant, Monty Python's
Spamalot, New York, NY (2004)

10

DIVINE INTERVENTION

In November of 1989, I had open heart surgery involving five arteries. At the time, the county office provided physical exams, called executives' exams, for all of its managers and the board of supervisors. These exams generally didn't involve a treadmill, but in the last week of August I was offered a treadmill test because it was a new part of the program. I definitely thought it would be advantageous to take the test, since it was new, and I certainly felt no trepidation about doing so.

I was still very active, including mowing my own lawn. I weighed 165 pounds, had no pain, and life was going along fine. I took the treadmill test at Doctors Hospital and was told I had passed it in terms of strength. However, I got a call about a half-hour later from a cardiologist who told me that he saw a little flicker in the test and didn't like it, and that we ought to go one step further.

That "one step further" would be a heart catheterization in the hospital in October. That's where they anesthetize your leg and go up an artery in the leg with a wire and take a look at the heart. The doctor's recommendation made me feel it was necessary to do the procedure to make sure everything was alright, but I certainly didn't believe I needed it.

The cardiologist came into the room after performing the procedure and said to me, "Ray, I hate to tell you this, but you are walking death. Are you sure you don't have any symptoms?"

I asked, "Why are you saying that?"

He said, "You've got coronary heart disease which, left untreated, most likely will lead to a heart attack. If you look here at your test results, your LAD — left anterior descending artery which is the largest coronary artery — is 98 percent blocked. I don't know how you are up and walking around. Your RCA — the right coronary artery — is 82 percent closed — serious enough to cause a great deal of trouble — and the three other smaller arteries that are obstructed aren't quite as significant, but they should be taken care of. With the LAD, we call what you have the widowmaker, because you could be walking around and suddenly drop dead, and everyone would ask, 'What happened to Ray Simon?' It is serious enough to tell you that it can come on spontaneously and probably will do so within the next several weeks. I am scheduling you to see Dr. James MacMillan, a cardiothoracic surgeon, immediately."

Well, I lay in the hospital that night because I couldn't move my leg; they had cut the artery quite severely. So I had time enough to think that they must be crazy, and I was going to ask for a second opinion.

Dr. MacMillan came in the next morning and showed me exactly what he was talking about. He said, "Ray, it's critical we schedule you for coronary bypass surgery without delay. You should have absolutely no trouble with this procedure because of your age, and I would say you are the perfect patient. Your health is good, you are lean, and you will fly through this operation."

Easy for him to say!

The next person I saw was Dr. Joe Neal, another heart surgeon, who was considered one of the best in Modesto. He was a very kind person and said to me, "For the coronary artery bypass surgery you need a quintuple bypass – that will include all five major arteries that feed into the heart. We do not plan to use arteries from your leg as a replacement, but your left mammary artery instead because that's much larger and will last longer. If it's possible, we will also use your right mammary artery, and that should make you fairly failsafe."

Well, Joan was with me, and we went home and decided that we should have a couple of coffees. It was around five o'clock in the afternoon of October 17th, and both of us were feeling rather depressed. As she fixed the coffee, suddenly I looked up and felt dizzy. Was this the beginning? Should I rush to the hospital? Or was it something else?

I began to panic. Then I saw that the chandelier was swinging back and forth from the ceiling. I looked out the window and noticed the pool water sloshing out of the pool from side to side, and our chairs were shaking.

Joan and I looked at each other and laughed. I said, "I'm not sick, it's an earthquake!" And sure enough, it was the devastating San Francisco Loma Prieta earthquake of 1989. We certainly felt it all the way over here in Modesto.

My heart surgery was scheduled for two days later. Of course I went to Doctors Hospital, and they began the preparations for my surgery. I remember the anesthesiologist was Dr. Gray Neuweiler, a very kind and reasonable man. He looked at me and said, "Are you worried about anything you want to discuss with me?"

I said, "Yes. The only thing I'm worried about is waking up with a tube down my throat and having a machine breathing for me for a while — in other words, being intubated."

He said, "I'll see what I can do. I have tried this certain procedure with some other patients, but if there is a detriment to your health after surgery, I will not remove it for a while."

Joan and the kids walked me to the door of the surgery room and waved goodbye. They were not allowed to touch me at that point.

When I came out of surgery five hours later, I was taken to the heart intensive care unit, and in came Dr. Neuweiler. "I succeeded in allowing you to breathe on your own without going into the intubation tube," he said, "and am very proud of myself."

Next, the cardiothoracic surgeon Dr. Neal came in and informed me that he had been successful in using the left mammary artery to sew into the area of the left anterior, and he was also successful in stretching the right mammary artery over. "You're one of the very few I've ever operated on who got both the left and the right."

Well, I was obviously weak, but they got me up and, with all the equipment tied to a pole made me walk around the room twice. The next day they brought me into a regular room, and I proceeded to walk around the hallways a number of times. I couldn't leave the hospital until I could walk the entire fifth floor five times in a row, and then they would let me out. It was a struggle, but I did it.

Once I got home, believe it or not, I was almost fully recovered within two weeks. I was up to walking two and three blocks at a time. I had again escaped a bullet.

———

The tragedy, in a way, of this story involved one of my best friends, superior court judge Eugene Azevedo. He had come in to see me when I was in the hospital in intensive care; I don't know how he got by the nurses, but that was Gene.

About six months later, I got a call at my office from his wife Marlene, who said that Gene had been taken to Doctors Hospital after experiencing a cluster of serious heart attacks. He wanted to talk to me and would allow only me to come and see him. So I rushed to the hospital, got to his room, and observed him in bed all black and blue in the face.

"Well, Ray," he began, "I had a number of heart attacks

today — one in the courtroom, in which they had to revive me; one in the ambulance, and they had to revive me again; one when I entered the intensive care unit in the hospital, and again they revived me; and once again in the room. I think that's enough."

I was astounded by the story and more astonished when he said, "Don't be afraid to die; passing through is the most peaceful thing I've ever experienced."

At that point, I looked at his chart, and since I had been in a similar position, I could see that his arteries were totally closed on both the right and the left.

I turned to him and said, "Gene, when are you having your surgery?"

He said, "I'm not having surgery. I don't want to look like you did when you came out of the surgery room. That was awful — painful and all kinds of stuff in and around you. That's terrible."

I said, "What kind of a fool are you? Do you realize that you are in serious trouble, and that my recovery after surgery was only five to eight days?"

Well, I could not reason with him. He didn't have surgery. He went home, and a week later, I heard him playing music in his backyard at eight o'clock in the morning, and back to drinking a full glass of bourbon.

I said, "You know you're going to die, don't you?"

He told said, "Ray, everyone has to die sometime."

It was our last conversation. That night or early the next morning, I got a call from his wife, Marlene. She said that Gene had died the night before in bed. He was 54 years old.

Almost all of my life I've been fairly free of illness. The next story I want to tell you happened after my retirement from the Stanislaus County board of supervisors. On July 18, 2017 – I remember it was a Tuesday – I went out to pick up the newspaper from the front porch. I reached for the paper, and the next thing I knew I had fallen down onto the concrete. I couldn't lift my arms and could not stand up.

I called out for Joan, and then seemed to fade away. The next thing I knew, two firefighters were standing me up, then sat me in a chair. They examined me quickly and said, "We can't find anything wrong."

The paramedics had also arrived. One of them looked at me and asked, "Mr. Simon, do you want to go to the hospital?"

I answered, "Yes."

From that point until after my arrival at the hospital emergency room, I don't remember much of anything. Everything I have to say about my first episode was relayed to me by my wife and son.

Apparently, I was taken to room 4225 after being examined in the emergency room. I was there for about two hours before my wife arrived. She tried to wake me up and couldn't. She told me later that I sounded very peculiar, so she called the nurse and said, "There's something wrong with my husband. He is wheezing."

The nurse said to her, "It's just a little congestion."

My wife said, "No, I want a doctor now."

The nurse told Joan to go sit down in the waiting room, and she would take care of it. While she was waiting, she heard over the loudspeaker, "Will all intensive care personnel report to room 4225." My wife knew that's where I was and walked down to look.

Joan saw a large number of people working vigorously on me, inserting tubes and a ventilator. Dr. R.J. Heck, a family practice physician, had arrived and he saw Joan. He came up to her and said, "Ray is extremely sick. I need your permission to use extraordinary measures to save his life." My wife asked him what was wrong with me.

Dr. Heck said, "His sodium is extremely low in his blood, and every time we give him sodium, it goes down further. He is close to death."

She naturally was in shock. He told her to call the family, because it might be close to the end. She left to do that.

There was a kidney specialist, the nephrologist Dr. Chang S. Joo, who stopped by the IC room I was in. According to my son, Dr. Joo asked the medical team, "You called my office, what's going on?"

They explained, and he said, "I know exactly what's happening and I need to run to the hospital pharmacy myself. I can't wait for the pharmacist to send it over, as it would be too late."

He left and came back with something — I cannot tell you what it was at this time. Whatever it was, they began injecting it intravenously, and in a short period of time my sodium levels started returning to normal.

From that point on, I began to recover — but they kept giving me tests to try to figure out what was wrong with me. I was given MRIs of my brain, lungs, stomach, and heart, along with a number of other tests. They could find nothing wrong and told me I was an extremely good shape.

Later I was able to ask Dr. Joo what it was that he had done. He told me, "We all have a hormone in our kidney that switches sodium on and off, and I knew all I had to do was to switch it on again for you."

Another divine intervention, that the one doctor who recognized this mysterious illness happened to be at the right place, at the right time. If Dr. Joo hadn't come along when he did, it's quite certain I would not have made it out of that room alive.

After a number of tests, it was decided that I should be admitted to rehab again to regain my strength and ability to walk; by now I had been lying on my back for nearly five weeks in the hospital. My doctor chose English Oaks, which had a relatively good reputation. However, they didn't have any private rooms. They put me in a room with two other gentlemen — in other words, it was a three-person room.

I was there for about three days when I realized that the rehab program was literally nonexistent. Not only that, but I had become very ill. The doctor came to see me twice while I was sick and told my family that he thought I was getting the flu. He would check on me again in a few days, as he was leaving for a convention.

By this time they had me packed in ice because of a high fever of 102°, my jaw hurt terribly and my teeth ached so bad I couldn't chew and it actually felt like they might fall out. Every meal I'd eaten that day came back up, and eventually I lost consciousness.

My son was there with me and said, "This is intolerable – and I can't reach Dr. Heck. I'm calling his partner, Dr. Forester." My son notified Dr. Forester he'd better come quick; they were not able to wake me up. Near death, the doctor had me transferred to Memorial Hospital via ambulance.

As I've been told, it was some time later that Dr. Forester arrived at the hospital. Jeff told him, "I feel it's important to bring this up to you, that Dad mentioned his toes were sore. He kept telling us his feet, his toes, were aching so badly that he couldn't stand it, and now he's complaining that his teeth ache so horribly, it's unbearable. I believe Dr. Heck has treated him for this before, and he said it was gout."

Gout is a complex form of arthritis, and can be indicated by acute, abrupt attacks of pain or sensitivity, swelling, and redness in the joints. Frequently it presents in the big toe, but in severe cases can affect any joint in the body, causing dull or sharp jaw and teeth pain and inflammation, and even teeth loss.

Dr. Forester asked, "What did Dr. Heck treat him with?"

"I believe it was prednisone, and Dad came right out of

it, he even regained consciousness."

Dr Forester immediately exclaimed, "My goodness. Knowing all of these symptoms, I know exactly what's wrong, and I'm going to fix it." He then told us that he had treated his father for this same incident twenty years ago. And that is when Dr. Forester diagnosed me with giant cell temporal arteritis.

The symptoms of giant cell temporal arteritis are similar to gout, but can include severe head and jaw pain, loss of vision or double vision, fever, and fatigue.

The strange thing about having temporal arteritis is that all doctors have heard or read about it but only a very minute portion have ever treated it. I also learned that I was going to have to take a small 5 mg tablet of prednisone every day for the rest of my life. No one knows what causes temporal arteritis, and the treatment is prednisone.

He hung the bag of liquid prednisone on the IV stand next to my bed and started the intravenous drip. An hour or so later, my eyes popped open suddenly and I saw that my kids were there. I asked them where I was and, "What are you doing here?" They explained what had transpired in the last few hours, and I told them "I've never felt so good. I feel like I have been reborn." I was free of pain and all of the symptoms.

Once I'd recovered, the doctor indicated he would like to send me to a different rehab facility, a brand-new hospital called Encompass Health Critical Care Rehabilitation Hospital of Modesto (formerly Health South). Their personnel came in, examined me, and their doctor on staff authorized my transfer.

There's no doubt that without Jeff's intervention, insisting that I go back to the hospital immediately and calling Dr. Forester when Dr. Heck was unavailable, I would not have survived.

This second rehab hospital, Encompass, was a great experience — private room, private bath, excellent physical therapy, a gymnasium with excellent therapists, and a wonderful cafe. At first, I used a wheelchair; I couldn't walk and would pull myself by my legs rather than using my arms as I went from my room to eat three meals a day. I went to physical therapy as well. When I was admitted, I had to agree to spend a minimum of three hours a day in physical therapy, which I was happy to do.

I spent three weeks there, and they got me back on my feet. I used a walker for a while when I got home and then graduated from the walker and finally was on my own. Two years later, I am still dealing with a balance problem of sorts, but I am otherwise healthy and able to fully function. That is why, after so many people prodding me to write my story, I decided to sit down and put pen to paper.

Since starting to write my memoirs there have been other more recent interventions. One in particular happened one evening when Joan and I had just finished dinner at Verona's as is our habit most Friday or Saturday nights. It was a beautiful June evening and when we walked to the car I didn't see the concrete parking block in front of my car and suddenly tripped right over it.

I landed on my knee and suffered a substantial cut over my knee cap.

Just at that moment a car pulled up and a man and woman jumped out. The man told me, "Don't stand up until I look at that." He had a small flashlight in his hand and lifted my pant leg up to the injury. He said "I will help you into my car. Have your wife follow us. I'm Dr. Basi and I will fix you up." He drove me to the large five story black glass building on McHenry Avenue and went inside to get a wheelchair for me. Once I recovered from my shock, I realized I'd gotten into a car with a stranger who claimed to be a doctor. You can imagine my relief to realize on the way to the medical facility that Dr. Basi was an absolute gentleman and gave me no real reason for concern. It had all just happened so fast.

Dr. Basi wheeled me into the building and I saw Elite Urgent Care stenciled on the glass door. You can imagine my further surprise when he produced a key to that door. He took me to the surgical room and his wife, whom he had told me was also a doctor, sterilized the area and anesthetized the wound. He cleaned the laceration and expertly sewed in 11 stitches to close it up.

I realized then that it was around 10:00 pm and he had opened the clinic for me out of pure goodness and consideration, plus he and his wife had missed dinner. Joan and I thanked the two Drs. Basi profusely and asked how much we owed them, but they would not let me pay. He said, "Just go home, take some Tylenol and get some rest."

I thought to myself that the timing of my accident and two doctors pulling up in time to witness it, these are two human angels. I called Verona's and gave them my credit card number and told them what had happened and that when the Basis come in for dinner, it's on me. Another divine intervention, and a chance this time to thank my angels in person. As well as their consequential rescue, Joan and I have enjoyed getting to know the Basis and they have seen us as patients, and we now know them as two first rate doctors in Modesto.

In conclusion, the most recent divine intervention to date is accidentally running into Al and Kim Spina, good friends of ours, at Verona's one evening a short time ago. Joan and I were enjoying a glass of wine when they walked by our table; they were being taken to be seated. Joan told them we hadn't ordered dinner yet and since we had a large booth, to please come and sit with us, and they accepted our invitation.

During the dinner course Al asked me what had I been up to in my retirement from the board of supervisors, and I told him I was writing my biography at the insistence of family and friends, and had hoped to have it printed by now. I mentioned my dilemma of getting my manuscript published after quite a long time in the hands of a publisher, and Al revealed that Kim is a first reader and edits manuscripts for authors, and why don't I ask her to help me with mine.

She accepted much to my delight, and besides polishing my manuscript she put me in touch with one of her associates, the incomparable Josie Brown (JosieBrown.-com), Author and Knower of All Things Publishing. Josie's expertise led to lifting the huge weight of the years-long publishing scam that had my project mired by unscrupulous frauds. Little did I know this inadvertent meeting would lead to moving my project to fruition.

Well over a year ago I'd given my original manuscript to a corrupt publishing company (actually well known as a scam/predator company that preys on people who aren't familiar with how publishing works) and was ready to give up getting my memoirs published. They wouldn't return my calls or my manuscript, and were charging me a monthly fee "for their services" to boot.

With this new information, my grandson who is an attorney was able to write a strongly worded letter to "cease and desist" and have them return the substantial amount of money they'd swindled out of me so far, and return my documents as well. As luck would have it, my most recent divine intervention.

———

When all is said and done, I have walked with angels most of my life, and they have been there to guide, help, advise, and ultimately save me.

I have always been convinced that when a baby is born, God sends the child's angel, and that angel follows the child through life. The angel is there through thick and thin, through good and bad. All you have to do is ask, listen, and believe.

Thinking back to how I first arrived at such an interest

in angels, my first thought was of my mother. All through my life, my mother was my strongest supporter.

Of the six children in our family I believe that for some reason she spent the most time with me, encouraging me to succeed in whatever I happened to be doing at the time, and she was the first to instill in me the importance of creating and attaining my goals. During every stage of my life that's exactly what I did, I followed her advice and would work on goals, never quitting until I reached that particular objective only to then move on to the next phase.

Even before I was born my mother had a sense about this new life she was bringing into the world. She felt she was having a boy, and that there was just something special about this baby she carried. She decided to name me after a popular movie star of that period, Ramon Navarro, and believed this feeling was a portent of what was to come.

At the early age of four she taught me to sing, and it turned out to be such a natural thing for me that she entered me in a singing contest one year later, which I won. Because of that performance, for the next few years I was called upon to sing in a number of cities for different organizations and events.

I remember my parents driving me to the Algeria Shrine Temple in Helena, Montana and I sang Christmas carols for the Algeria Shriners International convention, the Masonic Grand Chapter Order of Eastern Star, and a number of Rotary clubs.

When we moved to Portland, Oregon she sent me to a dramatic arts school hoping that I would become involved in theatre, which I did extensively. She taught me how to dance because she wanted to be sure I knew "how to dance with a lady," and she encouraged me to go to college eventually, because education was so important to her. I was the only person in my family to graduate from college.

In Modesto she urged me to run for the City Council when the opportunity was presented. She had great hopes for me throughout my life. She had, after all, named me Raymond after her favorite silent movie star.

One other thing that was very important to my mother was that I become a dedicated Christian, and she encouraged me to attend Sunday school each week, which I did. Oftentimes I went to church alone; no one else in my family was interested in attending church services, not even my parents. I didn't mind; I enjoyed listening to the various ministers and was mesmerized by the way they spoke and how they presented religious matters, even though I was not as focused on religion itself. It might sound strange, but that's how it was.

When all is said and done, I have walked with angels most of my life, and they have been there to guide, help, advise, and ultimately save me.

Angel pin given to Ray by Marie Gallo who told him, "God bless you, Ray. Wear this pin and it will always protect you."

Ray Simon, Stanislaus County Board Meeting (2006)

President George W. Bush's congratulations on
Ray's retirement from Stanislaus County Board of
Supervisors (2006)

Sheriff Lynn Wood appoints Ray as a Stanislaus
County Deputy Sheriff (2006)

Ray Simon Political Lion Award statue presented to Ray Simon, October 26, 2006 by MOPAC (Modesto Chamber of Commerce Political Action Committee)

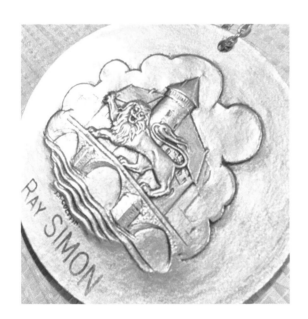

The French Senate awarded Ray this silver medallion for establishing Stanislaus County's twinning relationship with County Mayenne in France

Modesto Rotary Club, Distinguished Public Service
Award 2006

Ray and Joan, Opening of the Gallo Center for the
Arts

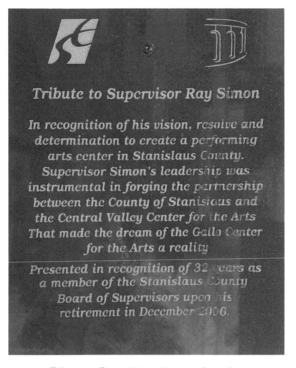

Tribute to Ray at his retirement from the
Stanislaus County Board of Supervisors. For his
36 years of leadership and guidance in realizing
the Gallo Center for the Arts (2006)

Gallo Center for the Arts, major contributors, Ray
and Joan Simon $250,000 (2006)

Ray in his office, holding down the fort

Ray at his 90th birthday party (2021)

PERSONAL

- Born in Conrad, Montana, 1931
- Married Joan Pedego August 31, 1958

We have two children:

- Our son Jeff Simon and his wife Tuesday Van Dyke Simon, and their three children Jessica (Dan), Christian, and Corbin, and two great-grandchildren Harper Rae Vella and Walker Hunter Vella.
- Our daughter Julie Simon Avery and her husband Greg Avery, and their three children Mathew, Cameron, and Courtney (John Piearcy).

CHILD ACTOR AT THE AGE OF 12

- Attended Broadway Director Donald Marie's School on acting, diction, and stage presence
- Toured with Summer Stock in 1944; WW2 Military Bases with stage production *The Tree and I* starring actors Ethel Barrymore and Edgar Buchanan
- 1955: Played male lead and Joan Pedego (Simon) played female lead in the MJC Theatre Arts, dramatics class production *Seventeen* with instructor Frank DeLamater

EDUCATION

- 1949 – Graduated from Missoula County High School, Missoula, Montana
- 1950 – USAF Aircraft and Engineer School, Sheppard Field, Texas
- 1956 – AA Degree, Modesto Junior College, Modesto, California
- 1958 – Bachelor's Degree, University of California, Berkeley, School of Criminology
- 1994 – Master's Degree, Bridgewater College, London, UK, under Chancellor of the Exchequer Criminal Justice Academy
- Thesis non-published: Successes and Failures of California's Three Strikes Law
- 1995 – Honorary PHD Criminal Justice, MacArthur University, London, UK
- European Registry Brussels, Belgium

MILITARY EXPERIENCE

- 1950-1954 – Staff Sergeant, United States Air Force, Korean Conflict
- Served in the Strategic Air Command as a B-29 Flight Engineer
- 1954 – Honorable Discharge

BUSINESS EXPERIENCE

1958-1960:

Under recommendation of Orlando Wilson, PhD, former OSS Western European Spy Commando, then Department Head of UC School of Criminology, I was recruited to enter a new program as a CIA Special Agent to work with the Congressional Un-American Activities Commission, the Seattle Public Schools and the Seattle Police Department to identify and report on the Russian infiltration into the schools to establish communist cells. 5 cells were established and a nationwide child pornography distribution group prosecuted.

1960-1994 – Investigator and Partner, Freese & Gianelli Claim Service

1994- Present – Chairman of the Board of the Simon Companies:

Pegasus Risk Management
Freese & Gianelli Claim Service
Status Bill Review
Status Medical Management
Status Investigations
Simon and Simon Investments

- 1987-1992 – Director, Modesto Banking Company
- 1998-2002 – Director, Modesto Commerce Bank
- 1998-2002 – Director, Stanislaus Surgery Center

ELECTIVE GOVERNMENT SERVICE

- 1964-1965 – Modesto City Planning Commissioner
- 1967-1976 – Modesto City Councilmember
- 1973-1974 – Vice Mayor, City of Modesto
- 1974-2006 – Stanislaus County Board of Supervisors, Fourth District, five times served as Chairman
- 1974-2006 – Chairman, Tuolumne River Regional Park System
- 1992-1993 – President, Stanislaus Cities and County Government Committee

APPOINTIVE GOVERNMENT SERVICE

- 1969-1974: Appointed by Governor Ronald Reagan to California Council of Criminal Justice
- 1970-1974: Appointed by California Attorney General Tom Lynch to head State Task Force on Law Enforcement, Education and Training to CCCJ (California Council on Criminal Justice). The Task Force developed the statewide Regional Criminal Justice Training Academics
- 1972: Nominee of the Republican Party for California Assembly, 30th District
- 1977-1978: Chairman, Regional Criminal Planning Board, Region K
- 1979-1980: Chairman, Stanislaus Area Association of Governments

- 1985-1994: Appointed by Governor George Deukmejian to the California Council on Emergency Services
- 1992-1993: Appointed by the Board of Corrections as Executive Steering Committee Member to revise California local detention facility standards
- 1995-1999: Appointed by Governor Pete Wilson to the California Board of Corrections
- 1998-1999: Appointed by the Board of Corrections as Chairman of the Executive Steering Committee for the Federal Violent Offenders Program

AWARDS

- 1967: Outstanding Young Man, City of Modesto
- 1975: Advisory Board of Editor's Outstanding Young Men of America, Junior Chamber of Commerce
- 1981: Named as one of the only three to ever receive Honorary status as a Firefighter, Modesto City Firefighters Local 1289
- 1982: Miss California Pageant Honorary Award for Service
- 1998: Regional Criminal Justice Training Center completed and named the Ray Simon Regional Criminal Justice Training Center
- 1998: Good Egg Award, Stanislaus County Farm Bureau and Egg and Poultry Association

- 2006: Silver Medal of Honor from French National Senate for work honoring French-US county to county relationships and twinning
- 2006: Appointed honorary Stanislaus County sheriff's deputy by Sheriff Lynn Wood, presented with sheriff's deputy badge
- 2008: Award by Cal Pac (California Pacific Conference); Chamber of Commerce Perpetual Award called the Ray Simon Award titled "Lion in California Politics" to Ray Simon, Supervisor, October 28, 2008

VOLUNTEER SERVICE

1965-1967
Chairman, Stanislaus County March of Dimes, two terms

1966
Founding President, Modesto Junior College Foundation

1967
County Chairman, Easter Seals

1968
Building Fund Chairman, YMCA

1969
Special Events Chairman, Boy Scouts of America

1976

Assistant Chairman, Central California Bill Graham
Crusade

1988

Advisor/Speech Coach, Miss America Pageant

1998

Chairman, Stanislaus County Heart Fund

ABOUT KIMBERLY GERBER SPINA, CO-AUTHOR

Kimberly Gerber Spina serves on the Stanislaus County Office of Education board, which she sees as a platform for championing alternative education programs for students who fit outside the usual educational "box," and mentoring youths, no matter their circumstance.

Understanding the importance of early language immersion motivated Kimberly to spearhead a Spanish/English dual immersion program in the Modesto City Schools' elementary school district. At the same time, through her educator friend Adele Little she met Debbie Mar who was just returning to Modesto, California after dedicating 12 years teaching at an elementary school in China. Together they brought a Mandarin Chinese language and culture program to Modesto City Schools' Enslen Elementary.

Her fervent wish for all public elementary students to have the opportunity to partake in music education at a time music programs were being dismantled inspired her to start a non-profit in 2008. The Salida Performing Arts Foundation brought an all-inclusive strings immersion program to Sisk Elementary School. A fundraiser in her home included former Secretary of State Condoleezza Rice playing the piano, Broadway tenor Dennis McNeil serenading, and world-renowned cellist Michael Reynolds, who each graciously contributed their time and talent to the foundation, which enabled Salida Arts to hire a strings specialist instructor and purchase over 100 violins for students, including a 1/10 scale modern acoustic violin tailored to the needs of a student affected by dwarfism as requested by his compassionate teacher.

Kimberly was honored as an Outstanding Woman of Stanislaus County in 2011 for her extensive volunteer services focused on children, founding Salida Performing Arts Foundation, launching an elementary string immersion program, and mentoring young disadvantaged children.

She is the wife of a walnut farmer/retired corporate executive and mother of two sons, in Modesto, California. She is enthusiastic about reading, writing, editing, and assisting authors to develop their story or fine-tune a manuscript.

It's with great gratification she has collaborated with Ray Simon to bring his life story to fulfillment.

ACKNOWLEDGMENTS

Walking with Angels could not have happened without family and friends' support and constant pestering to write my memoirs.

When I reached the point of writing my autobiography I began to reminisce about the various times that I had experienced a brush with death, and how those moments of certain demise were interrupted by divine interference; divine interventions that had been described to me by an elegant and articulate preacher named Johnny Lavender when I was a young boy attending his sermons regarding divine healings.

Lying in the hospital, near death due to serious complications resulting from low levels of sodium in my system, I was mostly comatose except for a brief period of time when I woke up in the intensive care room while Dr. Heck was calling my wife, expressing to her, "Ray is extremely sick. I need your permission to use extraordinary measures to save his life." I heard that and instantly thought to myself, *'The only way out of this now is if I have angels here to save me.'* An angel did come to me in the form of Dr. Chang Joo within 10 or 15 minutes of that desperate prayer.

Every event that happened to me in terms of nearly

losing my life came back to me and I began attributing my salvation to angels and divine intervention.

I look back with great pleasure at the experiences that made me, the loved ones who have unwaveringly surrounded and supported me, the acquaintances, colleagues, and collaborators with whom over the years I have joined forces, all the while staying true to myself, my values, and the path I had set for myself at a rather young age.

First, I must thank my family who encouraged me to put down in writing what I took for granted as simply the fun and memorable stories of my life, including my grand-parents, parents and siblings who encouraged my core values and helped me to grow into the young man I would become with their guidance.

I bestow my absolute and heartfelt thanks to Joan Pedego Simon, my beautiful, loyal, and devoted wife of 65 years; to have and to hold, for better, for worse, for richer, for poorer, in sickness and in health, to love and to cherish until we are parted by death, my stalwart companion and best friend for all of these years.

My son Jeff Simon and his wife Tuesday Van Dyke Simon, my health advocates and constant guardians during hospital stays, along with my daughter Julie Simon Avery and her husband Greg Avery, ceaseless in their love and support of my well-being in good times and bad.

My dear first grandchild Matthew Avery who has grown up to be so very like me. I am delighted to see the young man he's become, especially in his demeanor and unfaltering dedication to his career; Jessica Simon Vella, my granddaughter who cheerfully embraces my health management, and her husband Dan Vella who consistently inspires Jessica to her best and highest good; Christian Simon and Corbin Simon, my grandsons whose ceaseless antics keep me young; grandson Cameron Avery, whose adventures keep me on my toes and always looking forward to his next venture; granddaughter Courtney Avery, and her husband John Piearcy who has joined our family literally as this book of memoirs is going to press, their wedding reminding us of everything the future holds for young people in love; and great-grandchildren Harper Rae Vella and Walker Hunter Vella who are profound reminders of the miracle of life and a constant joy.

If I could, I'd reach out to all of my friends from the time I was a youngster, many of them already passed from this life, with whom experiences brightened and changed my life, including boyhood friends Bunny Norley and Tony Bannister; as a teenager my best friend George Jensen; my buddy Gary Nelson who palled around with me on Tarague Beach when we were stationed at Andersen Air Force Base, Guam; and my heroes Herbert Bronson, Red Dog Norley, and Captain Paul Aldhizer. It is my fervent wish wish that descendants of these true friends may come across this narrative so they can learn stories they may never have heard, that might give them another insight to their loved one long gone.

Louis "Bud" Gianelli, Attorney at Law, my closest friend and confidant, who was like a brother to me and became one of my most admired and cherished friends when I returned to Modesto. Bud was pivotal to my success as a young man starting my career.

To the medical specialists who became critical to some of the "divine interventions" which are central to this story: Dr. Joe Neal and Dr. James MacMillan, cardiothoracic surgeons whose insistence to continue tests tests I was sure I didn't need and didn't want, saved my life; Dr. R.J. Heck, family practice physician; Dr. Robert Forester, family medicine specialist; and Dr. Chang Joo, a nephrologist whose unanticipated entrance at the right place and right time, again rescued me from imminent demise.

The life changing experience of public service was made possible by the endless energy, advice, and support by those who worked diligently on my campaign for Stanislaus County Board of Supervisors: Mike Zagaris, CEO of Paul M Zagaris (PMZ) Real Estate, and George Petrulakis, Principal, Petrulakis Law & Advocacy, campaign advisors; Wilmar Jensen, Jensen & Jensen Attorney at Law, and Dr. Mark van Overbeck, campaign finance advisors.

As the years went by, I found myself feeling absolutely blessed by the many people I would call friend, including Michelle Zaldua, my personal secretary throughout my career; Reagan Wilson, Stanislaus County CEO; Michael "Mick" Krausnick, Attorney; Ray Nish, editor and Dave Cummerow, assistant editor, Modesto Bee; Federal Judge Frank Damrell; Superior Court Judge Paul Hanson; James Barnett MD, Interventional Pain Medicine Specialist; Bob and Marie Gallo; and Al and Kimberly Spina. Without the unexpected assistance of Kim Spina who came to my rescue when I thought the publishing of my memoirs was all but lost, and her husband Al who has supported and encouraged these efforts as well, this book might not have come to fruition.

And finally I must recognize Josie Brown, Kim's good friend and prolific author who, out of the goodness of her heart immediately came to the defense of a complete stranger, and succinctly informed me how the criminals who were stealing my memoirs could be brought to justice, stopped making unauthorized charges to my credit card, as well as return my manuscript to me along with money they had already swindled. With the help of my grandson, we wrote a letter to cease and desist and curtailed their illicit efforts. Josie eventually agreed to formally perform the specifics needed to convert my memories into an actual book, for which I am eternally grateful.

—Ray Simon

Printed in the USA
CPSIA information can be obtained
at www.ICGtesting.com
LVHW062333211123
764530LV00025B/472/J